MAXIMUM
PERFORMANCE FOR CYCLISTS

MAXIMUM
PERFORMANCE FOR CYCLISTS

Michael J. Ross, M.D.

BOULDER, COLORADO

Maximum Performance for Cyclists
© 2005 Michael J. Ross

Disclaimer
The information in this book is intended for educational and instructional purposes. It is not intended to replace medical care, rather to be an adjunct to it.

Printed in the United States of America.

10 9 8 7 6 5 4 3 2

Distributed in the United States and Canada by Publishers Group West.

Library of Congress Cataloging-in-Publication Data

Ross, Michael J.
    Maximum performance for cyclists / Michael J. Ross.
        p. cm.
    Includes index.
    ISBN 1-931382-62-X (pbk. : alk. paper)
    1. Cycling—Training. I. Title.
GV1048.R68 2004
796.6—dc22

                                                                    2004022973

VeloPress®
1830 North 55th Street
Boulder, Colorado 80301–2700 USA
303/440-0601 | Fax 303/444-6788 | E-mail velopress@insideinc.com

To purchase additional copies of this book or other VeloPress® books, call 800/234-8356 or visit us on the Web at velopress.com.

Cover and interior design by Anita Koury.
Cover photo (Ernie Lechuga, Jelly Belly® PoolGel™) by Casey B. Gibson.

To Wendy and Ben,
for putting a smile on my face every day

CONTENTS

PREFACE

Training fascinates me. Manipulating physiology to improve fitness amazes me. After athletes improve, they can regain lost confidence, feel empowered, and become happier as they succeed at an activity they love to do.

I have been coaching and training athletes for several years. During that time I have adopted different styles and techniques to accommodate various athletes. Two observations in particular have struck me: First, the peak power that people are capable of producing does not differ greatly from most amateurs to professionals. Second, what does change is the amount of time cyclists can maintain that power. To compensate for differences among athletes, training plans should be completely individualized. Individualization extends to the length of workout intervals and recovery nutrition to accommodate the difference among individual physiology. Just as two people have different size feet, no two individuals have exactly the same physiological make up.

> **To compensate for differences among athletes, training plans should be completely individualized.**

In this book, I will show you how to make a personalized training program. You will calculate intervals and nutrition to match your individual anatomy and physiology. If you follow this guidance, you will develop a training plan unlike any other.

This book abandons many of the long-held training notions that have no basis in science. Training in the second millennium should be based on science, not myth.

This is the second book I have written. If you have read the first (*Maximum Performance: Sports Medicine for Endurance Athletes*, VeloPress 2003) you know that I approach training and sports medicine as a science. I have studied the effects of different workouts on the body, and this book contains only those workouts and training that will help you improve.

Training goes beyond what you do on the bicycle. The benefits of training occur after you have put the bike away. It is important that you follow the pre- and post-workout nutritional guidelines as well. Recipes in the book will make this easy.

These principles have worked for amateur and professional cyclists alike. Read this book, learn some physiology, get on your bike—and become the best athlete you can be.

Go faster.

Michael Ross
Newton, Massachusetts

ACKNOWLEDGMENTS

I've been told that the second book is easier to write than the first. I suppose this is true about doing many things the second time around. This project would not have been so easy was it not for the support of several people:

Wendy for braving the first drafts and for your overall support that contributes to my general well-being

Ben for keeping me fit and sane with the constant game of "chase"

Justin for all the time spent in front of the camera

Michele and Ed for their comments and reviews

Jade Hays, Amy Rinehart, Rick Rundall, and Amy Walker for keeping things running smoothly at VeloPress

All of the athletes who have placed their health and fitness in my hands

My friends for understanding that I couldn't come out and play when they wanted to ride

Richard Bryne at Speedplay

Sandy Liman and Mark Landsaat at K2 bikes

Chris Zigmont and John and Mike Berlinger at Mavic

TRAINING OVERVIEW 1

VOLUME AND INTENSITY

Training volume and training intensity have historically been the two main variables in any plan to improve physical fitness. Volume refers to how much you train. Intensity refers to how hard you train.

Manipulating these variables has traditionally been the staple of any endurance program. The training season usually starts with high volume and low intensity. As training progresses, the volume decreases and intensity increases (Figure 1.1).

What if I told you there is a better way?

Only half of our training improves in fitness. The problem is to know which half. Whether that half is volume or intensity remains to be seen, but there is increasing evidence that intensity is the more important half.

If you increased volume and intensity together, you would surely burn out from physical exhaustion. If you increased only volume, you wouldn't see any significant improvement. If you train by manipulating intensity, you will improve.

Why, then, do we focus so much on volume? Tradition. That's the way training has always been done. The great racers used to do it. The great riders now do it.

Maybe the people who excel in a sport are the people whose bodies adapt well to traditional training. When I first started racing, I had coaches whose traditional plans developed national and Olympic champions. We did high intensity on Tuesday, Wednesday, and Thursday and then raced on the weekends. The people who improved with this schedule were the people who recovered well. There were only two days off—nonconsecutive days—per week.

INTENSITY AND RECOVERY

It's time to start thinking of training as manipulations not of volume and intensity but of intensity and recovery. Using training principles taken from the exercise-science research, you can maximize your improvements while optimizing your recovery.

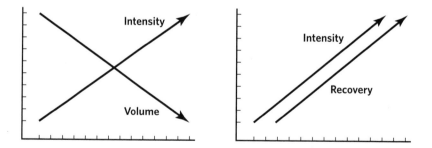

FIGURE 1.1 > The new training model: We used to think of training as a manipulation of volume and intensity; now we must think of training as a manipulation of intensity and recovery.

If traditional training has worked for you, then you already should have achieved great success in cycling. If you feel you could progress further, you should examine your motives for choosing workouts and building a training plan.

"Because it works for him" is an unproductive way to approach a training plan. Just because a plan works for the other guy doesn't mean it will work for you.

If you want to excel in cycling, you need to adapt the training to your body. I will show you how intensity and recovery can help you reach your goals.

How Intensity and Recovery Can Maximize Performance

Many systems in the body are affected by training. The changes that occur in these systems can either help you or hurt you. If you train well, the changes will help. If you don't, you will not improve and may even regress.

Proper training will improve the function of your muscles and the hormones that help them recover. Changes in the muscles that produce fitness are called the "training effect." The training effect must occur in all types of muscle fibers for you to improve as an athlete.

TABLE 1.1 Effect of exercise on the endocrine system

HORMONE	HIGH-INTENSITY TRAINING	LOW-INTENSITY ENDURANCE
Thyroid Hormone	↑	↓
Growth Hormone	↑	↓
Testosterone	↑	↓

If you train well, the recovery hormones (also called anabolic hormones) are maximized, allowing you to train harder the next day (Table 1.1). If you train with too much volume or not enough recovery, your recovery hormones will decrease and you will be unable to train as hard in your next session. You also won't improve and your performance will suffer.

THE TRAINING EFFECT: CHANGES IN MUSCLES
THAT IMPROVE PERFORMANCE

The power and endurance of the muscles must improve in order to maximize performance. There are three levels of power you need for bicycle racing: endurance, sustained power, and maximum power. Training with intensity improves performance in each area.

Endurance

Endurance has different meanings to different types of athletes. For recreational athletes, endurance might mean being able to go for a long distance at a slow pace. For racing athletes, endurance means being able to hold a lot of power for a long period of time.

Endurance is not a function of how many base miles (long, low-intensity riding early in the training season) you have logged but rather is a function of the size of your muscle fibers, how well you are able to supply them with energy, and how efficiently they use energy.

Muscle-fiber growth, energy delivery, and energy use do not happen with traditional base miles. In fact, base miles can even cause the endurance fibers to shrink. The new training paradigm suggests that along with appropriate interval training and weight training, you need to train the energy-storage and manufacturing systems in the muscles.

The training effect is achieved with a combination of intensity and recovery. During recovery, nutritional manipulations that are timed with workouts will train the body to store energy and use it more efficiently. Although what you eat during training and racing is important, what you eat after training and racing is more important. Well-planned recovery after well-planned workouts will keep you going longer and stronger.

Sustained Power

Whether climbing a hill or attacking your opponents, you need to have sustained power. This comes from muscle fibers that are powerful but that lack the long-distance ability of the muscle fibers primarily responsible for endurance. Like the endurance sections of muscle, the sustained-power muscle fibers are also trainable for use in energy storage and production. A combination of work and recovery through effort, rest, and nutrition will take you to the next level.

Maximum Power

The third component of the successful endurance athlete is the ability to employ maximum power over a brief period. This happens during sprinting, jumping away from your competitors, and climbing short hills. Because these fibers rely upon different energy sources, they are not as trainable as the other components with nutritional manipulations; rather, you must train at specific intensity to develop them.

THE COMPLETE PICTURE: BEYOND THE BIKE

Flexibility

The complete athlete possesses many physical characteristics. Power is important, but the body also must function well. Strength, endurance, and power are important but cannot be optimal without flexibility.

Increasing flexibility of your muscles and tendons is often overlooked during training; however, stretching exercises can lead to faster position on the bicycle and decreased risk of overuse injury.

As a complete athlete, you become dynamic. A perfect pedal stroke, bike fit, or position will change as you train, not only throughout the season but for specific events as well.

Strength

The distinction between strength and endurance athletes becomes blurred in high-intensity training, because it produces changes in the muscles similar to changes that occur with weight training. Weight training, combined with brief workouts to increase the training effect will not only make you stonger, but will strengthen muscle tendons and provide better recovery as well.

Nutrition

Nutrition will not help you if you are not training well, but poor nutritional habits can be detrimental to your training progress. Learning what to eat and when to eat it will take you a long way toward improved fitness. Several types of meals are important to athletes to improve recovery and efficient energy use:

3-to-1 carbohydrate and protein

The ratio of 3 grams of carbohydrate to 1 gram of protein is the key to ensuring adequate recovery. Your body needs protein to build and repair muscles and carbohydrate to fuel those muscles. The amount of carbohydrate is calculated based upon your weight. Carbohydrates are most effective for recovery when eaten immediately after training and then again at one hour after training.

High carbohydrate

High-carbohydrate meals are great for packing the muscles with stored glycogen as part of a carbo-load workout.

Low carbohydrate

If muscles are deprived of carbohydrate for three days during a recovery period, they will crave carbohydrate and will be more able to store carbohydrates when you reintroduce them into your diet. Focusing on a low-carbohydrate diet during the rest days that follow hard training can enhance the effect of training.

High fat

Following a high-fat diet for five days will teach the muscles to use fat as an energy source. Since fat contains twice the calories of carbohydrate, it is a useful fuel source for low-intensity exercise, sparing the carbohydrate for higher intensities.

SUMMARY ■ Traditional training involves a progression from high volume to high intensity.

■ High-volume training can decrease recovery and strength.

■ Know when to decrease your volume and replace it with intensity.

■ Intensity is the most efficient way to increase the training effect.

■ Intensity helps develop endurance, sustained power, and maximum power.

■ Recovery from intensity is the key to improvement.

■ Combining proper diet with exercise will increase recovery.

■ Flexibility, resistance training, and nutrition are all important for maximizing performance.

If you are looking for a training plan that will help to develop you as an athlete or if you are seeking to augment your existing training plan, the next few chapters will help get you there.

The Training Effect:
HOW TO INCREASE PERFORMANCE

2

CHANGE THE WAY YOU RIDE

Increased performance occurs through changes known as the training effect. These are changes in the muscles and the body that result in greater endurance capacity. As you train, the body adapts to the rigors of exercise by becoming stronger and more efficient. The training effect occurs on biochemical, cellular, and structural levels. Surprisingly, the best way to get the benefits of exercise isn't through long, slow endurance rides.

By identifying the specific changes that occur with the training effect, you can design workouts to target the specific response to exercise, making training more efficient. Specific changes that occur in the muscle include increases in the size, number, and function of the cellular energy factory, the *mitochondria;*[1] an increased number of blood vessels that deliver blood (and oxygen) to the muscle; and a transformation of muscle-fiber types.

While the changes in the muscles occur on a microscopic level, the heart and lungs also undergo a training effect that results in a stronger and more efficient way to pump blood to the exercising muscle.

All of these changes culminate in an increase in the maximum amount of oxygen that the body can use, and as oxygen use increases, so too does endurance capacity.

THE BIG PICTURE

The relationship between the heart and the muscle is like a distribution company (the heart) that has to supply different factories (the mitochondria within the muscles) with the raw materials needed (oxygen and glucose) to create energy.

With exercise there is an increased need for energy, the factories have to increase production. To meet this need on a regular basis, the existing factories will need to expand; and new workers will need to be hired. Within the muscles, the energy factories are called *mitochondria* (one factory is a *mitochondrion*). As the body adapts to exercise, the mitochondria get bigger, more numerous, and more efficient. Efficiency happens through an increase in the enzymes that carry out the energy-producing reactions.

When exercise intensity increases, so too does the demand for oxygen and glucose. As the demand increases, more raw materials must be distributed. There are several ways to do this. One way is to increase the roads that lead to the factories to provide more efficient delivery. In the muscles this happens through an increase in the blood vessels that supply the muscles with blood and oxygen, a process called *angiogenesis*.

These processes are not automatic. Knowing how to manipulate them is paramount to designing a training program.

Finally, the distribution center itself will need to expand. As walls are knocked down and rebuilt, more materials can be delivered with each shipment. As the shipments get bigger and more efficient, it is easier to deal with a larger demand. Like the distribution center, the heart expands and "remodels" itself, becoming bigger, stronger, and more efficient with training, pumping more blood with each heartbeat. At rest, the heart can pump fewer times, but with exercise, each larger and stronger heartbeat will deliver more oxygen, enabling you to go faster for longer periods.

MITOCHONDRIA

Every muscle cell in the human body relies upon energy to perform its job. Energy is manufactured in the mitochondria, a tiny organ within all cells. The mitochondria are the energy factories.

The more mitochondria present in any given muscle cell, the more energy the cell can generate. More mitochondria prevent fatigue and increase the ability to produce power at higher intensity. Indeed, increased mitochondria result in an increased aerobic efficiency.[2]

With an increase in mitochondria, the cell can make more energy and rely less on the energy reserves, called glycogen. This results in decreased lactic-acid production, less muscle fatigue, and improved performance.

Training for cycling is aimed at producing an overall increase in the mitochondria productivity. This increase occurs through an increase in the number and function of mitochondria (more numerous and more efficient factories).

The traditional low-intensity training method of progressively longer rides is one way to increase mitochondria. Low-intensity training, however, has a negative

What is lactic acid?

Lactic acid is a waste product of energy production. Lactic acid is always being made, but usually it is at a sufficiently low level that it is recycled into usable energy. As exercise intensity increases beyond a certain point, the production of lactic acid rises quickly. This point is known as the lactate threshold. Once the production of lactic acid begins to outweigh the use of lactic acid, you start to feel a burning in your muscles. Lactic-acid accumulation quickly leads to fatigue and decreased power.

effect on recovery. Most of the mitochondria synthesis occurs not during exercise but during recovery[3] from exercise with a peak synthesis of 18 hours after exercise.[4] Workouts that specifically target mitochondria growth can increase their function while allowing for proper recovery.

Increasing the Number of Mitochondria

The first priority in training is to increase the number of mitochondria. This entire process requires approximately six weeks to accomplish following any given workout.

The most potent stimulator of mitochondria growth is repeated muscle contraction. Almost any prolonged duration of repeated muscle use will start to increase the number of mitochondria. One exception to this rule is resistance exercise (weight training), which is too brief to be a potent stimulator of mitochondria growth. High-intensity training is the most efficient way to increase mitochondria because it recruits more muscle fibers. Mitochondria growth occurs only in muscle that is recruited (used) during exercise.

A continuous stimulus of exercise intensity must be provided to maintain the mitochondria. Mitochondria are made and destroyed every few days. Rapid increases in mitochondria are observed quickly with each new level of training. The downside is that without a continued level of training intensity, mitochondria disappear quickly after 10 days. Resistance training with weights can help prevent a decline in mitochondria performance.

Two factors in particular stimulate mitochondria growth: calcium and energy depletion. Calcium released from the cells during muscle contraction acts as a signal for the cell to make new mitochondria. Calcium should be present during exercise. Taking a calcium supplement prior to exercise may be useful. Avoid extended-release compounds, however, as they will minimize the amount of calcium available during exercise.

Energy depletion is a more potent stimulator of mitochondria growth than calcium. Energy is made from carbohydrate and oxygen. Careful training in the absence of either carbohydrate or oxygen will lead to rapid energy depletion.

Energy depletion can therefore be achieved with a ride that is done in the absence of carbohydrate at or just below the maximum aerobic function (lactate threshold heart rate—see Chapter 5 to discover this value for yourself). At this level, the maximum number of mitochondria-containing muscle fibers will be recruited. After the body has used up all of the energy, muscle breakdown will occur to fuel exercise. It is important to stop this workout before the body begins to break down muscle, which occurs at about one hour. If you feel that your power output is decreasing before one hour, you should end the ride.

The ride should take place first thing in the morning, after an overnight fast, so that the body has small carbohydrate reserves. If you are unable to ride first thing in the morning, it is still possible to deplete energy stores by riding at a moderate intensity for close to one hour without eating carbohydrate during the ride. After approximately 90 minutes, your glycogen stores will be depleted and you can add some intensity. Undertake intervals of increasing length (1, 2, 3, 4 minutes) until you are no longer able to produce power. After either one of these rides, it is important to replace both carbohydrate and protein at the 3:1 ratio (1 gram carbohydrate and 0.3 grams protein per kilogram of body weight). Specific workouts are described in Chapter 9.

Mitochondria Function

Increasing the number of mitochondria is one way of increasing energy production. Increasing the function of each individual mitochondrion is another way and can be accomplished faster.

Within the mitochondria, factory workers called enzymes carry out the conversion of glucose (from the food that you eat) and oxygen into energy. Studies have shown that in response to moderate-intensity exercise (2 hours a day for 7 days), enzymes increased by nearly 100 percent.[5] A 30 percent increase in enzymes decreased the amount of blood lactate and increased endurance performance by 10 percent.[6] After 5 days of training, enzyme activity increased 53 percent. At 10 days, the rate of mitochondrial energy production was 160 percent greater than before training. Interestingly, training beyond 10 days did not result in further increases.[7]

What is VO_2max?

VO_2max is a scientific term that represents the maximum aerobic potential. A higher VO_2max means that you can ride faster for longer than if you had a lower VO_2max. Regardless of what the number is, the most important aspect of training is how much power you can produce at VO_2max.

Measuring your VO_2max requires an expensive setup that measures the amount of oxygen that you breathe in and out during exercise. While having all of these parameters recorded, you increase your power every minute until you can't ride any harder. The highest level that you reach is your VO_2max.

It is possible to ride harder than your VO_2max, but this requires using your type IIb muscle fibers and can't be sustained. In this book, the term critical power represents the power at VO_2max. Chapter 5 discusses how to discover this value for yourself.

Increasing the function of mitochondria is easy to do and occurs quickly, and you do not need endless hours of mileage to achieve the desired effect. With just 2 hours of training a day for 5–10 days, it is easy to increase the function of the mitochondria. As exercise intensity increases beyond 80% of critical power (to determine your critical power, see Chapter 5), the increase in function becomes exponential.[8]

There are some pitfalls to be aware of, however. Iron deficiency can lead to a decrease in the function of the mitochondria.[9] It is important to maintain adequate iron stores with the supplementation of iron during muscle and mitochondria enzyme-building workout periods.

Although the increase in mitochondria enzymes can be accomplished in five days, there is a rapid reversal in one of the enzymes once exercise is stopped.[10] Most of the enzymes remain, however, and the decrease is prevented in individuals who have done strength training, even after 14 days of exercise withdrawal.[11]

Glycogen Depletion

Diet plays an important role in mitochondrial biogenesis. Changing your diet to suit the desired training effect will increase the productivity of your workout.

To be ready for exercise intensity, the body stores carbohydrate for fuel in the muscle in the form of muscle glycogen. Glycogen is also stored in the liver. Muscle contractions increase mitochondria growth, and intensity further increases their growth. When workouts are performed in the presence of glycogen depletion, the effect is even greater. Glycogen depletion can be achieved through several different workouts. If you exercise as soon as you wake up, your liver glycogen is already depleted from the overnight fast. Glycogen also is depleted as you ride, but exercise intensity determines the time required for depletion. You should not exercise on an empty stomach longer than one hour or you risk breaking down muscle protein for use as energy. One hour at 91% of VO_2max (critical power), which is slightly above lactate threshold heart rate, will deplete glycogen stores.[12] To perform this workout, stop when your power drops. Continuing beyond this point will lead to muscle breakdown.

Other factors that will lead to an increased rate of glycogen depletion include a lower-than-normal cadence.[13]

Glycogen depletion is an effective way to increase mitochondria both during and after exercise, provided it is done properly. Eating a low-carbohydrate, high-protein diet for three days after exercise will lead to increased mitochondria growth in the three days of rest following a training block.[14] It is important that you maintain protein intake and make sure that these are absolute-rest days, when you don't train at all. Trying to exercise without adequate carbohydrate stores will lead to inefficient workouts and muscle breakdown and set you up for decreased immune function and overtraining.

Angiogenesis

Another very important part of the training effect is developing new blood vessels that will deliver oxygen-rich blood to the mitochondria. Only through new capillaries can the muscle receive the raw materials necessary to transform oxygen into energy. The development of new blood vessels—called angiogenesis—occurs in the muscle as a result of exercise.[15] The capillaries receive chemical signals from even moderate exercise,[16] but there are specific types of training that can further increase angiogenesis signals.

The factors that specifically signal the body to increase angiogenesis are related to an increased need for oxygen delivery. They are low blood-oxygen levels, anaerobic exercise, and decreased blood flow. Of these, the easiest to control is exercise intensity, specifically anaerobic exercise above the lactate threshold heart rate.

Almost any exercise above the lactate threshold heart rate will generate a lack of oxygen sufficient to cause lactic-acid accumulation that is necessary for capillary growth.

As exercise intensity increases, you consume more oxygen to produce the necessary power. At a certain point, not enough oxygen delivery is available for the mitochondria to produce the maximum amount of energy. Further energy production in this state is made from stored muscle glycogen without oxygen. Once this happens, you are operating above the lactate threshold and are using anaerobic metabolism.

Almost any exercise above the lactate threshold heart rate will generate a lack of oxygen sufficient to cause lactic-acid accumulation that is necessary for capillary growth.[17]

In research studies, high-intensity endurance training, defined as 90 minutes of intense effort, was enough to induce capillary growth.[18] Short, intense bouts also induced capillary growth.[19] Intensity, not length, of exercise apparently accounts more for maximizing capillary growth.

HEART

The heart develops its training effect from an increased heart rate. With chronic elevations of the heart rate, as happens during training, an increased volume of blood reaches the heart compared with the at-rest state. Like a balloon filled with water, the walls of the heart will dilate (called dilatation), increasing the size of the heart. With a stretched balloon, however, the walls become thinner as the heart increases in size. To strengthen the thinning heart muscle, the walls of the heart thicken. The result is a stronger heart that can accommodate more blood. As the heart becomes more efficient, it will beat more slowly but still provide adequate delivery of blood. Although you do not feel the heart stretch and its walls thicken, you will notice your training leads to a lower resting heart rate.

For the body to incorporate these changes, the heart must be continually overloaded. If you exercise only at the same low heart rate, the changes will not occur. When exercise is performed near maximal heart rate, not only will the number of beats increase the volume of blood through the heart, but the heart also must increase the volume of blood it pumps with each beat to meet the demands of exercise. Exercise at close to maximal heart rate will induce a volume overload of the heart to ensure dilatation and wall-thickening.

SUMMARY ■ The training effect of increased mitochondria performance, increased mitochondria function, and angiogenesis can increase exercise capacity. Combined with the increases in heart function that take place with training for endurance exercise, this enables the body to become a more functional athletic machine.

■ Although exercise at less than maximum effort will produce some degree of change, the most significant heart improvements come as a result of intense exercise.

■ The training effect in the muscle causes an increase in blood delivery, energy production, and energy storage.

■ The mitochondria are the energy producers of the muscle cells.

■ Mitochondria increase from exercise in the presence of energy (glycogen) depletion.

■ Growth of capillaries, called angiogenesis, increases delivery of oxygen and energy.

■ Angiogenesis is best stimulated by intense exercise.

■ The heart adapts to the effects of training at an elevated heart rate.

NOTES

1. J.O. Holloszy. 1975. Adaptation of skeletal muscle to endurance exercise. *Medicine and Science in Sports* 7, 3 (Fall):155–64.

2. D.A. Hood. 2001. Invited review: Contractile activity-induced mitochondrial biogenesis in skeletal muscle. *Journal of Applied Physiology* 90 (2001):1137–57.

3. J.O. Holloszy and W.W. Winder. 1979. Induction of d-aminolevulinic acid synthetase in muscle by exercise or thyroxine. *American Journal of Physiology. Regulatory, Integrative and Comparative Physiology* 236 (1979): R180–3.

4. M. Takahashi, D.T. McCurdy, D.A. Essig, and D.A. Hood. 1993. D-aminolae-vulinate synthase expression in muscle after contractions and recovery. *Biochemical Journal* 291 (1993): 219–23.

5. E.A. Gulve and R.J. Spina. 1995. Effect of 7–10 days of cycle ergometer exercise on skeletal muscle GLUT-4 protein content. *Journal of Applied Physiology* 79, 5 (November):1562–6.

6. R.J. Spina, M.M. Chi, M.G. Hopkins, P.M. Nemeth, O.H. Lowry, and J.O. Holloszy. 1996. Mitochondrial enzymes increase in muscle in response to 7–10 days of cycle exercise. *Journal of Applied Physiology* 80, 6 (June):2250–4.

7. E.C. Starritt, D. Angus, and M. Hargreaves. 1999. Effect of short-term training on mitochondrial ATP production rate in human skeletal muscle. *Journal of Applied Physiology* 86, 2 (February):450–4.

8. G.A. Dudley, W.M. Abraham, and R.L. Terjung. 1982. Influence of exercise intensity and duration on biochemical adaptations in skeletal muscle. *Journal of Applied Physiology* 53, 4 (October):844–50.

9. D.A. Hood, R. Kelton, and M.L. Nishio. 1992. Mitochondrial adaptations to chronic muscle use: Effect of iron deficiency. *Comparative Biochemistry and Physiology* 101, 3 (March):597–605.

10. H.H. Host, P.A. Hansen, L.A. Nolte, M.M. Chen, and J.O. Holloszy. 1998. Rapid reversal of adaptive increases in muscle GLUT-4 and glucose transport capacity after training cessation. *Journal of Applied Physiology* 84, 3 (March):798–802.

11. J.A. Houmard, T. Hortobagyi, P.D. Neufer, R.A. Johns, D.D. Fraser, R.G. Israel, and G.L. Dohm. 1993. Training cessation does not alter GLUT-4 protein levels in human skeletal muscle. *Journal of Applied Physiology* 74, 2 (February):776–81.

12. N.K. Vollestad and P.C. Blom. 1985. Effect of varying exercise intensity on glycogen depletion in human muscle fibres. *Acta Physiologia Scandinavia* 125, 3 (November):395–405.

13. L.E. Ahlquist, D.R. Bassett Jr., R. Sufit, F.J. Nagle, and D.P. Thomas. 1992. The effect of pedaling frequency on glycogen depletion rates in type I and type II quadriceps muscle fibers during submaximal cycling exercise. *European Journal of Applied Physiology and Occupational Physiology* 65 (4):360–4.

14. P.M. Garcia-Roves, D.H. Han, Z. Song, T.E. Jones, K.A. Hucker, and J.O. Holloszy. 2003. Prevention of glycogen supercompensation prolongs the increase in muscle GLUT4 after exercise. *American Journal of Physiology, Endocrinology, and Metabolism* 285, 4 (October):E729–36. Epub June 10, 2003.

15. T.L. Haas. 2002. Molecular control of capillary growth in skeletal muscle. *Canadian Journal of Applied Physiology* 27, 5 (October):491–515.

16. H.T. Yang, R.W. Ogilvie, and R.L. Terjung. 1998. Exercise training enhances basic fibroblast growth factor-induced collateral blood flow. *American Journal of Physiology* 274, 6 Pt 2 (June):H2053–61.

17. N.K. Stepto, D.T. Martin, K.E. Fallon, et al. 2001. Metabolic demands of intense aerobic interval training in competitive cyclists. *Medicine and Science in Sports and Exercise* 33 (2001):303–10.

P. Mucci, N. Blondel, C. Fabre, C. Nourry, and S. Berthoin. 2004. Evidence of exercise-induced o2 arterial desaturation in non-elite sportsmen and sportswomen following high-intensity interval-training. *International Journal of Sports Medicine* 25, 1 (January):6–13.

18. D. Gute, C. Fraga, M.H. Laughlin, and J.F. Amann. 1996. Regional changes in capillary supply in skeletal muscle of high-intensity endurance-trained rats. *Journal of Applied Physiology* 81, 2 (August):619–26.

19. I.J. Polakowski, E. Skopinska-Rozewska, K. Nazar, H. Kaciuba-Usciolko, and J. Langfort. 1989. Effect of endurance and "sprint" physical training on lymphocyte-induced angiogenesis in rats. *Folia Biologica (Praha)* 35(1):45–9.

MUSCLE PHYSIOLOGY 3

MUSCLE FIBERS AS AN EXERCISE GUIDE

Over the past twenty years, the different ways for an athlete to measure intensity have increased. The training tools we now take for granted were once available only to laboratory researchers and required large, expensive equipment. Initially we could measure distance and time, then speed. Shortly after, heart rate became an invaluable training parameter. Now we can measure power output, global position, and altitude.

If I were to be granted a wish of the most basic and useful meter for guiding exercise, however, I would choose a muscle-fiber recruitment monitor. All other monitors measure how hard we are working, but the bottom line is that they all provide an indirect measurement of how we are using our muscle fibers.

There are three types of muscle fibers. Each fiber type is associated with a particular intensity, a particular fuel source, and a particular power output. Understanding the connection among these different parameters will allow you to use intervals as a powerful training tool.

The training effect occurs only in muscle fibers that are activated; knowing the levels at which to train becomes very important if you want to see improvement in your performance.

With different muscle fibers, the body uses different nutrients to generate energy. Some fibers use oxygen, some don't. Some fibers can use fat for sustained energy, whereas others can use only carbohydrate.

Each fiber type has a particular activation level. If you are not working above a particular level, you won't activate that fiber type. The training effect occurs only in muscle fibers that are activated; knowing the levels at which to train becomes very important if you want to improve your performance.

MUSCLE-FIBER TYPES

There are three distinct muscle-fiber types. When you start any activity, the smallest and weakest fibers are used first. As exercise increases in intensity, larger fibers are recruited. There is not a shift from one type of fiber to the next; rather, recruitment is a continuum along which larger, stronger fibers are added to help the smaller ones.

The first muscle fiber to be activated for any activity is the type I fiber. This fiber is the smallest type and therefore has the weakest peak force. Type I fibers are also called slow-twitch because their contraction speed is the slowest. Despite their relative weakness and slowness, they can contract repeatedly over long periods of time without fatiguing; these are the fibers that will allow you to ride for several hours at a time.

Type I fibers rely on fat and carbohydrate as fuel during exercise. Below 60% of maximum effort, fat is the predominant fuel source for type I fibers. As more type I fibers are recruited, carbohydrate takes over as the main fuel source. The fat stored in type I fibers gives the muscle a darker or "red" appearance. This is analogous to the dark meat in a chicken, which is the chicken's type I muscle.

Fiber types and energy systems

The body manufactures energy in the form of adenosine triphosphate (ATP). This is a molecule that can be broken down for use in muscle function. Different fibers have the ability to create different amounts of ATP.

Type I fibers use fat and carbohydrate to create energy. This reaction occurs with oxygen and is called aerobic. One molecule of fat generates significantly more ATP than a molecule of carbohydrate. But the conversion of fat to ATP takes longer, so fat isn't useful for quick bursts of energy. The aerobic conversion of carbohydrate to ATP produces 100 fewer molecules of ATP than does the aerobic conversion of a similar-sized fat molecule, but carbohydrate is responsible for the majority of energy used during moderate or intense exercise. The quicker availability of the carbohydrate conversion process makes carbohydrate a better source of fuel.

Type IIa fibers use both aerobic and anaerobic metabolism. The body switches to anaerobic metabolism when the oxygen demand is greater than delivery. This happens at exercise intensities where you noticeably breathe harder. The byproduct of anaerobic metabolism is lactic acid. The point where you switch from aerobic to anaerobic metabolism is the "lactate threshold."

Aerobic metabolism produces over 16 times more ATP than anaerobic metabolism, but anaerobic metabolism is useful when there is insufficient oxygen delivery.

Type IIb fibers are only anaerobic and are unable to produce power for the long term. Although their peak force is high, they can produce power only for a short period of time (usually 10–15 seconds.) The main source of energy is the pool of creatine phosphate that is easily depleted after approximately 10 seconds. Each molecule of creatine phosphate makes only one molecule of ATP; the process thus is very inefficient, but the ATP is immediately available for high-intensity exercise.

Oxygen is needed for processing the fat and carbohydrate to be used as an energy source. If you are breathing easily during training, you are using primarily type I fibers. When your exercise intensity outweighs the supply of oxygen, all of your type I fibers are being used. You know all of your type I fibers are being used when the intensity nears the lactate threshold (see "What is lactic acid?" in Chapter 2).

As exercise intensity progresses, you start to breathe harder, and the fast-twitch fibers become involved. The first of these is the type IIa muscle fibers. They have a contraction speed faster than the type I fibers and produce power that is five times the force of a slow-twitch contraction (Table 3.1). Like the type I fibers, these are resistant to fatigue—they can sustain high power output for several minutes. These fibers are responsible for a late-race surge, a steep-hill climb, or a race-winning attack. Winning bicycle races is largely dependent upon

TABLE 3.1 Properties of different muscle fibers

PROPERTIES	TYPE I	TYPE IIA	TYPE IIB
Contraction speed	Slow	Fast	Fast
Color	Red	Red	White
Easily fatigued	No	No	Yes
Relative peak force	1	5 times type I	10 times type I 2 times type IIa
Energy source	Fat, carbohydrate	Carbohydrate	Carbohydrate
Utility	Endurance	Short, powerful efforts & the last part of long efforts	Sprints
Sustained work time	Hours	Minutes	Seconds
When recruited	Immediate	Moderate; primarily used up to 80% of peak aerobic function	Last; activated at 80% of maximum effort

being able to produce high power over the last few minutes of the race. Race performance depends upon the quality of type IIa muscle fibers. These fibers can function in moderate and hard efforts and can use both carbohydrate and fat.

Race performance depends upon the quality of type IIa muscle fibers.

Because of their versatility, high force production, and resistance to fatigue, these are the fibers to develop for bicycle racing. These fibers have the largest growth and recruitment during interval training and resistance training. An effort that you can sustain for 4–5 minutes primarily uses type IIa fibers.

Type IIa fibers are showing increased importance in long endurance rides as well. As you start to run out of energy for the type I fibers, the type IIa fibers contribute to the long, low-intensity effort.[1]

As exercise approaches 80 percent of maximum capacity, the type IIb fibers join the effort.[2] These fibers cannot use oxygen or fat. Because they lack stored fat, they are white. They have a high contraction speed and produce a force twice that of type IIa fibers and 10 times that of type I fibers. That force cannot be sustained for very long, however. These fibers are easily fatigued. If you are breathing heavily and exercising near your maximum effort, you are predominately using type IIb fibers. Brief bursts of intense, powerful energy, such as for a final sprint, use type IIb fibers. Their use can last up to 15 seconds, and the muscles usually require a period of complete recovery.

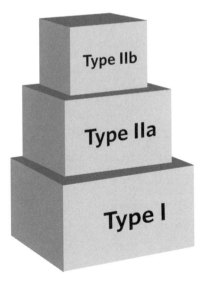

FIGURE 3.1 > Pyramidal use of different muscle fibers

The use of the muscle fibers is like a pyramid (Figure 3.1). To ascend the pyramid, you start on the lowest layer of bricks. As you climb to the next level, you are relying upon all of the bricks from the level below as well. The same is true with muscle fibers; with each new level, all fibers beneath that level are being used.

FIBER TYPES AND EXERCISE

Each fiber type is used during different parts of racing and training. Type I fibers predominate during light-intensity, long exercise. If you have ever been at the end of a long ride and are unable to go hard, you have probably exhausted your fuel for the type II fibers and are riding at the limit of your type I fibers. You would be unable to produce any intensity if you had only type I fibers. Even a long endurance event, however, still requires type II fibers for climbing hills or riding into the wind.

Whether you are charging up a hill, trying to break away, or accelerating toward the finish line, you are recruiting type II fibers. Type IIa fibers will power your hard efforts for 4 or 5 minutes before becoming fatigued. Once exercise intensity passes 80% of VO_2max, you need the help of the type IIb fibers. These are most often used during rapid attacks, sprints, or sudden accelerations.

EFFECTS OF TRAINING

Different types of training will have different effects on the various muscle fibers. Training does not cause new fibers to develop, but it does cause existing ones to grow larger. In addition, one fiber type can be transformed into another. Because there are no new fibers, transformation to one fiber type comes at the expense of other fiber types.

Weight training will induce transformation from type IIb fibers to type IIa fibers.[3] Furthermore, weight training will cause a growth of all muscle-fiber types.

Fiber types and cycling speeds

The speeds of cycling track records demonstrate the use of muscle-fiber types.[1] The record for the 200-meter (200m) flying start is 72.99 kilometers per hour (km/h) and took only 10 seconds. This effort relies primarily on type IIb fibers. As the distances increase, there is a switch to primary use of type IIa fibers. The 1,000m and 4,000m events were achieved at speeds of 61.15 and 57.34km/h, a difference of less than 4km/h, even though the distance is four times as great. As the events get longer and use mostly type IIa and type I fibers, the speeds do not continue to decline appreciably. The speeds in the 200m and 4,000m events differ by 16km/h, but the difference between the 4,000m and 1-hour records (56.38km) is only 1km/h even though the distance traveled is 12 times as long (Figure 3.2). Both of these events are largely aerobic, use similar muscle-fiber groups, and produce similar speeds.

As you can see, whether you train type IIb with interval training, or rely upon low-intensity endurance training, the result will be similar speeds for longer events, but training the type IIb muscle fibers will result in increased power and increased endurance.

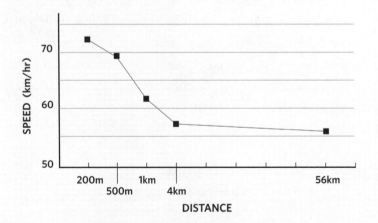

FIGURE 3.2 > How muscle-fiber type recruitment affects cycling speeds

NOTES:
1. Records obtained from Union Cycliste International (www.uci.ch), as of January 5, 2004

Interval training also will cause a type IIb to type IIa transformation as well as an increase in the ability to generate energy within the fibers.[4] Interval training also causes an increase in the type I fibers.[5]

Low-intensity endurance training, on the other hand, can promote a transformation from type II to type I fibers. This transformation occurs at the expense of the type II fiber population.[6] This does not mean that you should avoid low-intensity endurance training completely. Endurance training will increase the effectiveness of the fibers' contractions and energy production, but be careful not to overdo it. Prolonged endurance training can cause shrinkage of the type I and IIa fibers.[7] Because prolonged low-intensity endurance training can have a negative effect on fiber size, it is wise to keep the length of low-intensity sessions limited (2 hours a day for 10–21 days of total training).[8]

The most important factor to remember about muscle is that maximal exercise recruits all fiber types.[9] Only the muscle fibers that are recruited will show any benefit from training. Type I fibers are the primary fuel for low-intensity endurance exercise and rely upon fat and carbohydrate for fuel. Type IIa fibers provide high power for a prolonged period and are the most versatile in their use of energy. Type IIb generate the most power but only for 15 seconds.

To generate lasting power, you need to cultivate the type II fibers. To do this, you should train at high intensity so that the fibers will be recruited, trained, and strengthened.

SUMMARY ▪ There are three types of muscle fibers.
Type I fibers are responsible for long, low-intensity riding.
Type IIa fibers power intense efforts that last for several minutes.
Type IIb fibers are used during very powerful but short efforts.

▪ As intensity increases, all of the type I fibers are used, and type IIa fibers are added.

■ With further increases in intensity, type IIb fibers are added to the type I and IIa fibers. Maximal intensity recruits all fiber types.

■ Training effects are seen only in muscle-fiber types that are recruited.

NOTES

1. P. Krusturp, K. Soderlund, M. Mohr, and J. Bangsbo. 2004. Slow-twitch fiber glycogen depletion elevates moderate-exercise fast-twitch fiber activity and O_2 uptake. *Medicine and Science in Sports and Exercise* 36, 6 (June):973–82.

2. G.A. Dudley, W.M. Abraham, and R.L. Terjung. 1982. Influence of exercise intensity and duration on biochemical adaptations in skeletal muscle. *Journal of Applied Physiology* 53, 4 (October):844–50.

3. R.S. Hikida, R.S. Staron, F.C. Hagerman, S. Walsh, E. Kaiser, S. Shell, and S. Hervey. 2000. Effects of high-intensity resistance training on untrained older men. II. Muscle fiber characteristics and nucleo-cytoplasmic relationships. Journals of Gerontology. Series A. *Biological Sciences and Medical Sciences* 55, 7 (July): B347–54.
Tanaka, and T. Swensen. 1998. Impact of resistance training on endurance performance: A new form of cross-training? *Sports Medicine* 25, 3 (March):191–200.

4. P.B. Laursen and D.G. Jenkins. 2002. The scientific basis for high-intensity interval training: Optimising training programmes and maximising performance in highly trained endurance athletes. *Sports Medicine* 32, 1 (March):53–73.

5. Laursen and Jenkins 2002.

6. R. Thayer, J. Collins, E.G. Noble, and A.W. Taylor. 2000. A decade of aerobic endurance training: Histological evidence for fibre type transformation. *Journal of Sports Medicine and Physical Fitness* 40, 4 (December):284–9.

7. R.H. Fitts, and J.J. Widrick. 1996. Muscle mechanics: Adaptations with exercise-training. *Exercise and Sport Science Review* 24 (1996):427–73.

8. R.L. Terjung. 1976. Muscle fiber involvement during training of different intensities and durations. *American Journal of Physiology* 230, 4 (April):946–50.

9. Terjung 1976.

BIKE FIT 4

One principle of ergonomics is that the machine should be designed for the user, not that the user should have to fit the machine. Most bicycle components are designed to fit the user in three places (handlebars, pedals, saddle), but there are actually six contact points (left hand, right hand, left foot, right foot, left buttock, right buttock). How these six points are arranged in relation to one another dictates how efficiently the muscles can work to maximize power while minimizing injury. Even if power output isn't your main goal, the chances for injury are decreased with a properly fit bicycle. A good bike fit will lead to greater comfort and an increase in power.

Although not everyone has a custom frame, everyone can have a custom fit. Careful study of your anatomy, flexibility, and strength can help you create a bicycle fit that will grow with you. There are several factors to consider when properly fitting a bicycle: foot arches, leg-length discrepancy, Q-angle, flexibility, shoulder width, riding style, injury patterns, pelvis width, and arm length. A detailed analysis of each factor should be performed so that your body can achieve unity with the bicycle.

To perform an appropriate fit you will need the following tools:

- Tools needed for bicycle adjustment (4, 5, and 6mm Allen wrenches)
- Level 18–24 inches long
- Plumb line with weight
- Goniometer or protractor

A goniometer (Photo 4.1) is a device that measures angles by means of two legs that swivel around a central pivot. It can be found at medical supply stores.

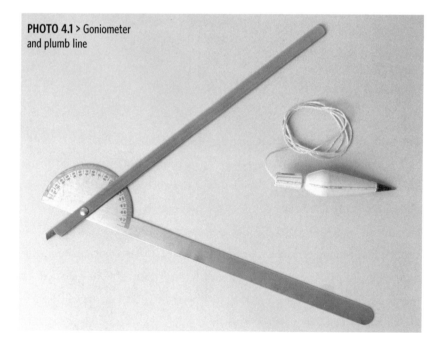

PHOTO 4.1 > Goniometer and plumb line

NINE STEPS FOR A CUSTOM BIKE FIT

Step 1: Determine the Need for Arch Support

The arch of the foot affects how the ankle, shin, knee, hip, and back interact. Feet that lack supporting arches roll inward, causing unnatural rotation of the shin (tibia), knee, and hip (Photo 4.2).

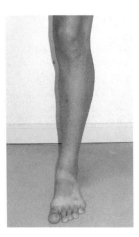

Weak arches predispose the cyclist to overuse injuries that affect the medial (inside) part of the leg. In contrast, high arches tend to affect the lateral (outside) part of the leg. A high arch also tends to be more rigid and provide less cushioning than a normal arch and can cause stress injuries such as plantar fasciitis and shin splints.

PHOTO 4.2 > Flat feet cause the knees and hips to point inward.

What is your foot type?

A normal arch provides cushion and support for the foot during a lifting-off or pushing-down activity (taking steps, leg press, or the downward force during pedaling). The arch is made up of numerous ligaments and provides a spring from which the next step or upstroke is launched. The normal foot also receives some shock absorption from the movement of the bones. Through the biomechanical processes of pronation (rolling in) and supination (rolling out), the foot can act as both a shock-absorbing cushion and a stable platform for launching the next step.

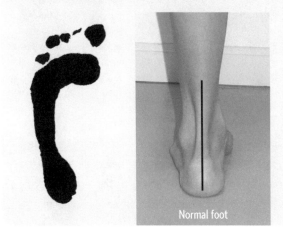

FIGURE 4.1 > **Normal foot:** In the normal foot, there is equal pressure on the outside of the foot and the inside of the foot. The Achilles tendon and the heel are aligned.

Normal foot

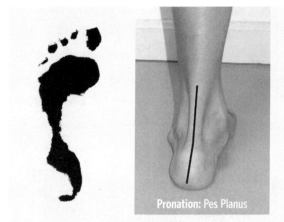

FIGURE 4.2 > Pronated foot: In the pronated foot, the weight of the foot is shifted toward the inside of the arch and off the outside edge of the foot. The top of the heel points inward with respect to the rest of the foot. The result is a poorly supported arch.

Pronation: Pes Planus

Pronation occurs as the foot rolls inward. Some pronation is normal because it helps the foot absorb shock as it strikes the ground. Flat feet cause overpronation. If a foot is excessively pronated, the feet, knees, and hips are affected. This leads to a decrease in power to the pedals. If your knees move from side to side as well as up and down during the pedal stroke, you are probably a pronator.

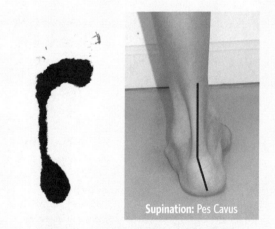

FIGURE 4.3 > Supinated foot: In the supinated foot, the weight of the foot is mostly on the outside edge of the foot. As the foot rolls to the outside, the heel points to the outside. The result is a poorly cushioned foot.

Supination: Pes Cavus

An arch that is too high becomes rigid and loses the ability to act as a shock absorber. Some degree of supination is necessary during the gait cycle to provide a rigid platform from which to push off. Supination occurs as the foot rolls to the outside. This places stress on the lateral ligaments and can lead to tendinitis.

To determine whether you need arch support, take impressions of your feet by creating wet footprints. To make a wet footprint, cut open and tape together several brown paper bags (or use a length of brown wrapping paper) and place the paper on a firm surface; you want a long sheet of brown paper on the floor in front of you. Next, rub petroleum jelly onto the soles of your feet. Now stand on the paper bag. I will refer to the impression that your feet leave as the *standing footprint*. From this position, take a few steps forward along the paper. The impressions left by your walking feet are the *motion footprint*.

Examine your standing footprint. It will likely fall into one of the three categories shown in Figures 4.1–4.3: normal, pronated, or supinated.

STEP 2: CLEAT POSITION

Before clipless pedals, shoes were attached to the pedals by cleats that did not rotate. Before cleats could be attached to shoes, it was extremely important that the heel rotation was correct. Thanks to the rotational adjustment provided by today's clipless pedals, this is no longer an issue. There are three adjustments in which the cleats can be set: heel rotation, forward-backward position, and side-to-side position.

Arch support

Once you have determined the need for arch support, you have several options available. Over-the-counter inserts are inexpensive but might not fit your foot if your toes are longer or shorter than average.

Custom insoles (orthotics) provide support exactly where your foot needs it and might be the only option if your feet are abnormally shaped. There are several methods for creating orthotics. You should consult your podiatrist to find out which option is best for your needs.

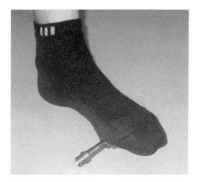

PHOTO 4.3 > Ball of foot over pedal spindle (shoe removed for clarity)

Step 2a: Setting the Fore-Aft Cleat Position

In the neutral position, the cleat should be aligned so that the ball of the foot is over the pedal spindle (Photo 4.3).

Moving the cleat forward on the shoe (moving the foot back on the pedal) will allow for increased movement of the ankle. By increasing ankle dorsi-flexion and plantar flexion, the muscles of the calf are lengthened, allowing for a more powerful upstroke as the calf muscles contract (Photos 4.4a, 4.4b).

However, if you have decreased flexibility in your calf muscles, you will want to move your cleat farther back on the shoe (foot farther forward on the pedal) until you can increase flexibility of the calf muscles (for calf stretches, see Chapter 8). To determine your calf flexibility, stand with the ball of your foot on a step and let your heel hang down (Photo 4.5). Repeat this test with the

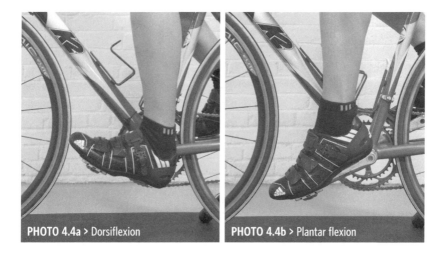

PHOTO 4.4a > Dorsiflexion

PHOTO 4.4b > Plantar flexion

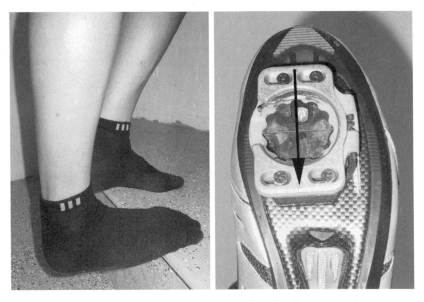

PHOTO 4.5 > Calf flexibility   **PHOTO 4.6** > Foot forward on pedal

other foot. A dorsiflexion angle of less than 20 degrees (measured with your goniometer) suggests decreased flexibility.[1] See the flexibility tests at the end of this chapter for other ways to test calf flexibility.

If you have decreased ankle flexibility, moving your foot farther forward on the pedal can be helpful (Photo 4.6). This position will take tension off the Achilles tendon, an important consideration for cyclists who have had Achilles tendinitis in the past.

Step 2b: Setting Cleat Rotation

Do your feet point in or out? Look at your wet motion footprint from the steps you took. Are the toes parallel with the direction you are facing, or do your feet point in or out? Even if the feet are pointing straight ahead when you are standing, they might point in or out during walking or pedaling. If your knee ever hits the bicycle during pedaling, your feet probably point in too much.

FIGURE 4.4 > A line from the base of second toe through the heel indicates the direction of the foot. Note the angle formed between this line and the direction you are facing.

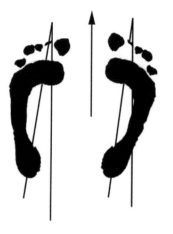

To determine the correct setup, measure the rotational angle of each foot with respect to the direction you are facing. When you set up the cleat on the shoe, replicate this angle. Finally, you should adjust rotation based upon previous injuries: Knee pain on the outside of the knee should prompt you to adjust rotation so that internal rotation (heel out) is limited. Similarly, inner knee pain can be corrected by decreasing external rotation (heel in).

Float adjustment

Once you have set your cleat position, determine the need for float. If your heel moves only a little, there are two possibilities. First, there is very little need for float and you do not need to make an adjustment. Second, the cleat pedal system is holding your foot in an unnatural position. In this case, not only will you feel that your foot is being pulled in a different direction, but your knees likely will start to move side to side as well as up and down to compensate. If that occurs, change your cleat rotation so that you do not feel the tension and your knees move only up and down. Repeat the test until you are comfortable.

If there is a lot of heel movement, you should adjust your cleats so that you do not point your toes inward excessively. Internal rotation may cause certain knee problems. If your knee hits the top tube, you probably toe in too much. If your pedals have rotation control, you may wish to decrease the float so that there is less energy wasted in foot rotation.

Once you have adjusted the float, make sure that your knees move only up and down and not in circles.

Step 2c: Side to Side—The Q-Angle

Most of the attention in bicycle fit is limited to the sideways view (up and down, fore and aft). Traditionally, little thought has been given to the frontal view, but it should be addressed to take hip width and foot stance into account.

PHOTO 4.7 > Measuring the Q-angle

A rider with wider hips often uses the same foot stance as a smaller rider, which can lead to injuries and decreased power.

If you were trying to hit a nail into a piece of wood with a hammer, you would hit it straight down, not diagonally. Similarly, if you were trying to transmit the maximum amount of force to the pedals, you would want to push straight down on the pedal. One way to determine that you are pushing down on the pedals most efficiently is by measuring the Q-angle.

The Q-angle is measured as the intersection between two lines. The first is the line from the bony prominence above the hip through the kneecap. The sec-

Fixing the Q-angle

If the Q-angle is larger than 22 degrees, the knees will be positioned such that the femur is not pushing directly down on the tibia. An increased Q-angle reduces downward force to the pedals and increases sideways force. The sideways force is wasted en-

ergy. A large Q-angle results from a difference in the width of the hips compared with the feet.

If the Q-angle is large, the feet must be widened relative to the hips. To accomplish this, the cleats can be moved to the inside of the shoes (see

Moving cleats to inside of shoes

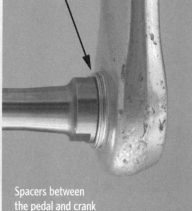

Spacers between the pedal and crank

ond is the line from the bony prominence below the kneecap through the kneecap. The intersection of these lines is important in the function of the knee (Photo 4.7).

To measure the Q-angle, have someone align the center of the goniometer at the center of the patella while the leg is at the bottom of the pedal stroke. Place one end of the goniometer along the patellar tendon and point the other end at the hip. The Q-angle should be between 10 and 22 degrees.[2] Keeping the angle at the lower end of this range will better align the leg to produce power to the pedals.

photo). If this still does not reduce the Q-angle sufficiently, spacers can be placed between the crank and the pedal (see photo on page 40) or a pedal with a longer spindle can be used (see photo below).

If the Q-angle is small, the feet are probably being widened unnecessarily. This may be the case with a smaller rider on a mountain bike or a knock-kneed rider. To remedy this, move the cleats as far to the outside of the shoes as possible (feet closer together) without the heels hitting the cranks.

Longer pedal spindles

Step 3: Determine Your Leg Length

Not everyone has a symmetrical body. Usually one leg is longer than the other. Sometimes this can be such a small difference as to be of little significance. Other times, the difference between the two legs can lead to a decrease in power, an injury, or both.

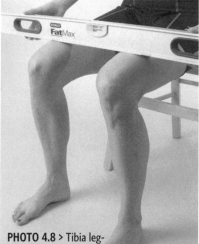

There are two stages in determining leg-length discrepancy. For the first test, you will need a carpenter's level that is at least as wide as your hips. Sit in a hard chair on a hard floor. Rest the level across the top of your knees. Any unevenness shown on the level is due to a leg-length discrepancy in the shin (Photo 4.8).

PHOTO 4.8 > Tibia leg-length discrepancy

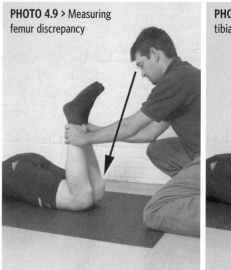

PHOTO 4.9 > Measuring femur discrepancy

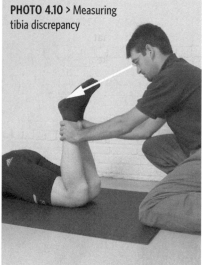

PHOTO 4.10 > Measuring tibia discrepancy

If the bubble in the level tips to one side, the differential should be measured with the help of a friend (Photos 4.9–4.10). Lie face down. Have your friend look at your ankles from above to examine for a discrepancy in overall length. Next, bend your knees to 90 degrees and observe if the knees are aligned (thigh length). Also measure the difference in the height of the heels (calf length).

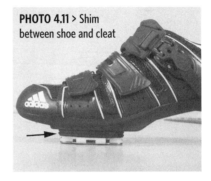

PHOTO 4.11 > Shim between shoe and cleat

If the overall discrepancy is greater than 6mm, a shim should be placed between the sole and the cleat. Some pedal companies make shims that can be used for this purpose. If the pedals you use don't have this option, you will need to cut shims from plastic sheets or use washers to provide space between the shoe and the cleat (Photo 4.11).

Step 4: Adjust Seat Height

Numerous formulas have been applied to inseam length and saddle height. I do not believe that any one particular seat height is the best at all times. In fact, seat height, like any component of the bike fit, should be fluid and change with an individual's needs, riding style, and injuries.

When the foot is at the bottom of the pedal stroke, the seat height should result in 25–35 degrees of knee flexion. Measure the knee angle so that the angle measures the variation from straight, not the angle between the thigh and the calf (Photo 4.12).

You should also select a seat height that will cater to your riding style. If your ideal cadence is high and you like to turn an easier gear, keep the saddle on the lower end of the range. Similarly, if you push a larger gear, set your seat height at the higher end of your range.

PHOTO 4.12 > Measuring the flexion angle

Seat height explained

Different angles created by the height of your bike seat will produce different results. If you set the seat height so that the knee forms a smaller angle (higher seat), you will be able to transmit more power to the pedals. A larger angle (lower seat) conserves more muscle energy, as the muscles do not have to work as hard to move the pedals in a circle. This position is better for spinning.

Shim the shoe

The seat height also affects the biomechanics of the knee. The more you bend your knee, the greater the stress placed upon the patellar tendon. If you are prone to pain in the front of the knee, maintain a smaller knee angle (higher seat). Conversely, if the muscles in the back and the side of the thigh are tight, they can cause iliotibial band friction syndrome if the seat is too high. If these are your particular problems, keep a larger knee angle (lower seat).

Occasionally, a seat height will result in big differences in knee angles between your left and right sides even though no leg-length discrepancy was measured. This can arise from a functional discrepancy in leg length. A functional discrepancy in leg length could occur from an old injury, muscle imbalance, or decreased flexibility on one side. If you have this discrepancy, add a shim to the pedal on the side with a smaller knee angle (see photo).

Step 5: Adjust the Seat Fore-Aft

Seat position can affect your riding style and power output. To find the best position for you, place the seat in a neutral position. From the neutral position, hang a plumb line from the tibial tuberosity (Photo 4.13). The line should fall at or just behind the pedal spindle and the ball of the foot (Photo 4.14). This position reduces the strain on the patellar tendon during the downstroke.

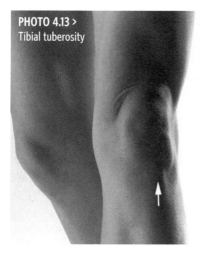

PHOTO 4.13 >
Tibial tuberosity

PHOTO 4.14 > Plumb line from the tibial tuberosity falls just behind the pedal spindle

A former coach of mine used to move the seat as far back as possible to give his riders more power. Although a seat position farther aft will give a more powerful pedal stroke because of the increased extension of the leg, the straightened leg can cause the same problems as a seat that is too high.

Remember, the bicycle should fit you, not the other way around. Seat position should be tailored to your riding style. If you tend to spin at a higher cadence, move the seat slightly forward; if you prefer to push larger gears, move the seat slightly back.

Step 6: Readjust the Seat Height

After moving the seat, check the knee angle again and adjust the seat height accordingly to preserve the knee angle you need.

Step 7: Determine Handlebar Width

Handlebar width is a matter of preference. A narrower handlebar is more aerodynamic and more responsive than a wider bar. Wider bars can be more comfortable and more stable for steering. Handlebars should not be any

Assessing hamstring flexibility

To measure hamstring flexibility, sit on a chair with your back flat against the back. Straighten one leg until the knee is straight and the ankle and hip are bent at 90 degrees. In this position, you should be able to keep your pelvis firmly planted on the chair and your back against the wall. Repeat with the other leg.

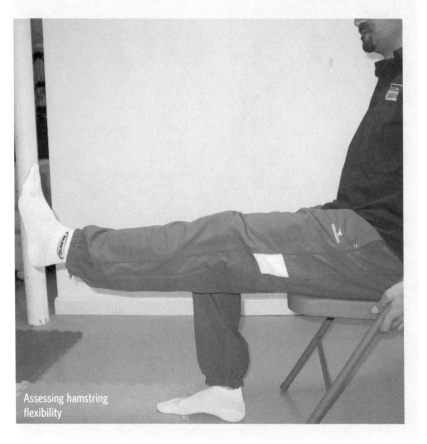

Assessing hamstring flexibility

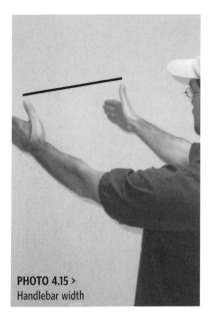

PHOTO 4.15 >
Handlebar width

narrower than the distance between your hands held straight out in front of you with your thumbs pointed to the ceiling (Photo 4.15).

Step 8: Determine Handlebar Height

Handlebar height is primarily a function of hip flexibility and core strength. A lower handlebar will allow you to maintain a greater bend in the hips, which will in turn result in increased power from the gluteus muscles in the buttocks. The angle of the hip, however, should not be artificially increased past a comfortable point. To measure the angle of comfort in the hip, lie on your back on the floor while a partner holds your leg and bends your hip until resistance is felt. Measure the angle made between your thigh and back. Set the height of the handlebars so that the angle is not any smaller when your hands are in the drops.

Another method of setting up the handlebars is to find the body angle at which you can hold a plank for one to two minutes. If one position is difficult, try resting your elbows on platforms of different heights (Photos 4.16, 4.17).

Back problems can be treated with small changes in handlebar height. Increasing the handlebar height will decrease the amount of work the back muscles perform. This also will alleviate pressure on the hands, which is a helpful strategy in treating numb and tingling fingers.

The ideal handlebar height may be difficult to achieve due to relatively weak core strength. Refer to Chapter 7 on weight lifting for examples of abdominal and back strengthening exercises.

PHOTO 4.16 > Plank

PHOTO 4.17 > Plank on platform

Step 9: Determine Handlebar Reach

Like handlebar height, reach is a function of core strength and comfort. The same hip angle should be maintained. If the reach is too far or your back and abdominal muscles are not strong enough, you will find yourself creeping forward and resting uncomfortably on the nose of the saddle.

To determine handlebar reach, copy the position of comfort in the plank test (see Appendix at end of this chapter). If you can support your weight with your elbows under your shoulders, the reach of the handlebars should approximate that position (Photo 4.16). If your weight is supported with your elbows in front of your shoulders, you can extend the reach.

Extending the reach because you expect to be more aerodynamic will only pull you forward on your saddle, decreasing comfort and power.

SUMMARY ▪ The bicycle should be adjusted to fit your anatomy.

   ▪ Fit should occur for each contact point on the bicycle.

   ▪ Your feet absorb all of the energy from the pedal stroke, so support them adequately.

   ▪ Proper angles of the knees and hips will allow for maximum power transfer.

NOTES

1. B. Anderson and E.R. Burke. 1991. Scientific, medical, and practical aspects of stretching. *Clinics in Sports Medicine* 10, 1 (January):63–86.

2. M.S. Juhn. 1999. Patellofemoral pain syndrome: A review and guidelines for treatment. *American Family Physician* 60 (1999):2012–22.

3. C.B. Corbin. 1984. Flexibility. *Clinics in Sports Medicine* 3,1 (January):101–17.

CHAPTER 4 APPENDIX

Flexibility and Strength Tests
Calf

To test calf flexibility, stand at arm's length from a wall. With feet at shoulder's width, place your palms against the wall and slowly bend your elbows, lowering your upper body to the wall (Photo 4.18a). When your forehead is against the wall, your knees should be straight and your heels on the floor.[3] If you are unable to place your forehead to the wall, try the test with each leg separately to see if there is a difference in calf flex bility (Photo 4.18b).

PHOTO 4.18a PHOTO 4.18b

PHOTOS 4.18a/b > Calf flexibility test

Measuring ITB flexibility: The Ober test

The iliotibial band (ITB) is a thick tendon that runs along the outside of the leg from the hip to the knee. The Ober test assesses the flexibility of the ITB. To perform the test, lie on your side with the bottom leg bent 90 degrees at the hip. The top hip is straight and the knee is bent. Relax the top leg. The knee should fall to the ground (see photo). If your knee hangs above the table or floor surface, you have a tight ITB and are predisposed to ITB friction syndrome (a common overuse injury on the outside of the knee); lower the saddle height to 30–35 degrees of knee flexion.

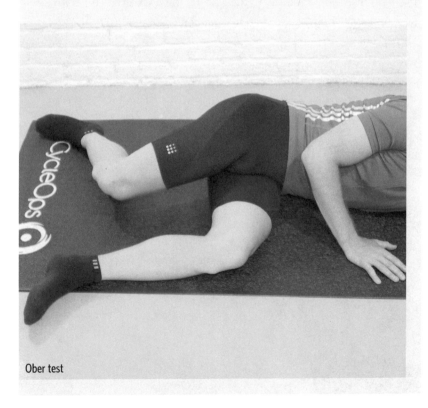

Ober test

Hamstring

Tight hamstrings can affect your entire position, decreasing your ability to become aerodynamic. To measure hamstring flexibility, sit in a straight-backed chair or on a table with your back against the wall. Let your knees hang off the chair. If you can straighten each leg without sliding your bottom forward or leaning back, you have adequate hamstring flexibility and can set a lower handlebar height.

Core Strength

A good test of core body strength is an exercise called the *plank*. To do the plank, kneel on all fours with your forearms on the floor. Next, push your body off the floor with the body resting on the elbows and toes (Photo 4.16). Contract the abdominal muscles and back muscles to keep the body in a straight line from your head to your heels. Do not allow your buttocks to sag. Time how long you can hold the plank, then adjust the handlebar/saddle differential based on Table 4.1.

TABLE 4.1 Plank and handlebar height

TIME	RESULT	RECOMMENDATION
Less than 1 minute	Fair	Minimal handlebar/saddle differential
1–2 minutes	Good	Several-centimeter differential
More than 2 minutes	Excellent	Set handlebar height as low as you can tolerate without your knees hitting your chest

TESTING

To train well, you have to know how hard you are working, and then track your improvement. Frequent testing tells you at what intensity to train and lets you follow your progress. By performing physiological tests, you can find appropriate training zones, training intervals, recovery times, and ideal cadence. Taken together, these variables will allow you to train more efficiently.

When testing, there are many different parameters to measure: power, speed, heart rate, cadence, and breathing rate. Commercial power meters can measure most of these. Although some of these tools have sophisticated software, all you need is a good assistant, basic power information, a heart rate monitor, and pen and paper. The three tests I find most useful are measuring for lactate threshold heart rate, critical power, and ideal cadence.

LACTATE THRESHOLD HEART RATE: THE MODIFIED CONCONI TEST

The point at which the body switches from predominately aerobic exercise to predominately anaerobic exercise is the *lactate threshold*. A simple test to determine the heart rate during the transition from aerobic to anaerobic was described in the early 1980s.[1] Since then, numerous variations of the protocol have been described, some with better results than others, but the initial test still remains valid.[2] The name of the test comes from the researcher who first described its utility. There are different results for different sports, with a higher lactate threshold for running than for cycling.[3]

Performing the Modified Conconi Test

1. Start the test after 2 days of rest and after at least 3 hours since you last ate solid food.
2. Set up the bicycle on a trainer with a power meter or rear-wheel speed sensor. If you have a cadence sensor, attach it. Wear a heart rate monitor.
3. Warm up for 15 minutes or until a light sweat forms on your legs.
4. Most athletes prefer to have a fan nearby.
5. Have an assistant record heart rate and cadence every minute.
6. Have your assistant note when your breathing becomes labored or your breathing rate increases.
7. Start pedaling at 60 watts.
8. Increase power output by 10 watts every minute.
9. Continue to increase power until your power output levels off or begins to decline. The highest power that you obtain is called the *critical power*.

Interpreting the Modified Conconi Test

After the test, plot the heart rate data versus power. You will end up with one of three lines: a straight line, a zigzag-shaped line with the final segment pointing up, or a zigzag-shaped line with the final segment level or pointing down. Figures 5.1–5.3 show examples.

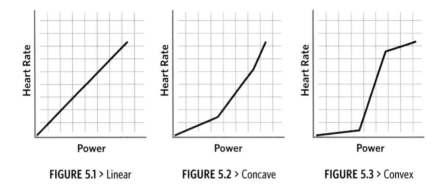

FIGURE 5.1 > Linear   **FIGURE 5.2 >** Concave   **FIGURE 5.3 >** Convex

The heart rate at which the final segment of the line bends is the heart rate deflection point. This point closely approximates the heart rate at which you change from largely aerobic to largely anaerobic metabolism.

There is another important point on the charted line. The heart rate also has a deflection early on. This point, known as the *aerobic threshold,* is where you really start to use the aerobic system. Below this heart rate, you are getting little training-effect benefit and are in recovery.

For the straight line, determining the lactate threshold heart rate is a little more subjective. Your breathing rate increases as you change from aerobic to anaerobic metabolism. The point at which your partner marked your increase in breathing is the *ventilatory threshold,* and the heart rate that corresponds to this is your *lactate threshold heart rate.*

If you have a straight line, plot your cadence to determine the aerobic threshold. You can use the heart rate at which your cadence started to increase as the aerobic threshold.

CREATING HEART-RATE TRAINING ZONES

You now have two heart rate numbers, your aerobic threshold heart rate (ATHR) and your lactate threshold heart rate (LTHR). Complete Table 5.1 by using the following steps:

TABLE 5.1 Determining your heart rate training zones

ZONE	LOW	HIGH
1	Resting heart rate:	ATHR:
2		
3		
4		LTHR:
5		Maximum heart rate:
80–85		

Following the steps outlined in the chapter, fill in the table with the values that you have calculated from your testing session.

1. Write your ATHR (aerobic threshold heart rate) as the high end of zone 1.

2. Write your LTHR (lactate threshold heart rate) as the high end of zone 4.

3. Divide the difference between the LTHR and the ATHR by 3 and use that number of heartbeats for each zone: Subtract LTHR – ATHR= _____ .

4. Divide the number from step 3 by 3: _____ ÷ 3 = _____ .

5. Add the result from step 4 to the ATHR and place this number as the high end of zone 2.

6. Add the result from step 4 to the high end of zone 2 and place this number as the high end of zone 3.

7. The final zone is the 80–85 zone. Multiply the highest power level you obtained (critical power) by 0.8 and note the corresponding heart rate. This is the low end of the 80–85 zone.

8. Multiply the highest power level you obtained (critical power) by 0.85 and find the corresponding heart rate. This is the upper end of the 80–85 zone.

Using the Heart Rate Training Zones

You have now created five distinct heart rate training zones for heart rate. Each of these zones is based upon different physiological states.

Zone 1 is recovery. The low end of zone 1 is your resting pulse. This is your heart rate when you are lying in bed in the morning. To get this heart rate, put on your heart rate monitor after waking up in the morning. Go to the bathroom and get back into bed. After a few minutes, check your heart rate; this is your resting heart rate. You are in a recovery state when your heart rate is between resting heart rate and aerobic threshold.

Zone 2 is a light aerobic zone. Training in zone 2 should be done with a high cadence. This zone will train your type I (slow-twitch) muscle fibers.

Zone 3 is a moderate-intensity zone that is the limit of your aerobic system. When exercising in this zone, you are maximizing your fat-burning capacity. You are also using all of your type I fibers. This zone should correspond to the maximum effort you are able to sustain at the end of a long ride when your carbohydrate reserves are empty.

Zone 4 is the anaerobic threshold. The fast-twitch, powerful fibers are starting to be recruited. Training for muscular endurance happens at this heart rate zone.

Zone 5 is all anaerobic. At this zone, all of your slow-twitch fibers are being used, and most of your fatigue-resistant fast-twitch fibers are being used. The powerful, fatigable fibers are recruited here as well.

Zone 80–85 is an important point along the critical power graph is 80% of critical power. This is where the type IIa fibers are maximally recruited, making this a benchmark for training. At this point, you are using all of your type I and type IIa fibers. The SPAM intervals that you will be doing are in this zone.

CRITICAL POWER OUTPUT

The maximum oxygen utilization (VO_2max) is the benchmark for endurance capacity. Determining the VO_2max is difficult and requires expensive equipment. The critical-power measurement provides similar information that has more useful applications for training.

Performing the Critical-Power Test

1. From the results of the modified Conconi test, note the power at which you stopped increasing your wattage; this is your critical power.
2. Keeping the same setup as with the modified Conconi test, start pedaling and try to reach the maximum wattage as quickly as possible.
3. Have your assistant record your heart rate every 5 seconds.
4. Continue to sustain the maximum wattage as long as you can.
5. Stop when the maximum wattage begins to decline.
6. Note the time that you were able to sustain maximum wattage until the decline of power.
7. Graph the heart rate against time.

I like to run the critical-power test shortly after the Conconi test because the setup is there and you are already warmed up.

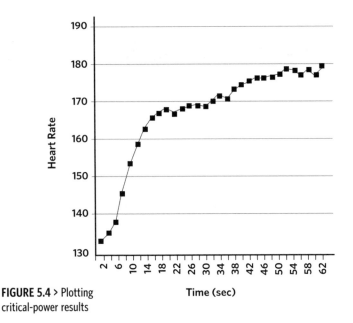

FIGURE 5.4 > Plotting critical-power results

Interpreting the Critical-Power Results

Graph the heart rate against time; you will have a curve that resembles the one in Figure 5.4. Look at the heart rate where the curve changes slope. This should be the same as the LTHR that you determined earlier.

Write down the number of seconds that you were able to sustain maximum wattage. This is your Tmax. Complete Table 5.2 for the different percentages of your Tmax. These are the high-intensity training (HIT) intervals.

An important percentage of critical power is 80% of critical power. This is where the type IIa fibers are maximally recruited, making this a benchmark for training. To calculate 80% of critical power, follow these steps:

1. Multiply critical power (watts) by 0.8: critical power x 0.8= _____ .

2. Look at the modified Conconi graph for the heart rate corresponding to the number in step 1.

TABLE 5.2 Tmax and high-intensity training intervals

TMAX	SECONDS	PERCENTAGE OF TMAX
50% Tmax	(Tmax x 0.5)	
60% Tmax	(Tmax x 0.6)	
70% Tmax	(Tmax x 0.7)	
80% Tmax	(Tmax x 0.8)	

IDEAL CADENCE

For every set of conditions (terrain, wind, grade), there is an ideal cadence and gear ratio that will allow you to move the fastest with the least amount of effort.[4] This concept of cycling economy will let you focus on a range of cadences that can help you ride faster while conserving energy. An ideal cadence will depend upon the type of riding you are used to, and will also vary with your muscle composition.

Knowing your ideal cadence is important because cycling with a less than ideal cadence will increase the stress on the muscles and the perceived effort of a ride.[5] Increased pedaling rates do not result in large increases in heart rates;[6] yet increased pedaling rates can greatly increase power output.[7] Although most experienced riders have a cadence around 90 revolutions per minute (rpm) on flats and 70rpm on hills,[8] climbing hills with a higher cadence will save energy and let you ride at a lower heart rate.[9] Testing yourself is the only way to discover your optimal cadence. The range of cadence that cyclists use is about 20% above and below the natural cadence. Use the following steps to determine this range and the ideal cadence within this range.

Testing for Ideal Cadence

1. Set up the bicycle on a power trainer with cadence as in the previous tests.

2. Do a 3-minute ride at 80% critical power.

3. Record your average cadence and average power over the ride.

4. The cadence you maintained is your freely chosen cadence (FCC)= _____ .

5. Multiply the FCC by 0.8 = _____ . This is the low end of your optimal cadence range.

6. Multiply the FCC by 1.2= _____ . This is the high end of your optimal cadence range.

7. On separate days do 3-minute intervals at the low end of your cadence range and at the high end of the cadence range. For example, if your FCC is 100, the low end is 80 (100 x 0.8) and the high end is 120 (100 x 1.2). Try a 3-minute interval at 80. The next day, do a 3-minute interval at 120.

8. Record the average power for each ride.

Interpreting Cadence-Testing Results

The ranges chosen for this test (FCC +/- 20%) correspond approximately to the range of cadences habitually used by road-racing cyclists.[10] The purpose of the test is to compare a naturally selected cadence with higher and lower ranges. If the power in the higher-cadence range was greater than the power for the FCC, you need to train with a higher cadence.

If the FCC test yielded the most power, then you probably are already using a cadence that works well for you. If this is the case, try to keep close to that range, even when riding uphill.

Definitions

Critical power: During a modified Conconi test, you increase your power every minute. You will eventually reach a point where your power no longer increases. This is the critical power.

Tmax, maximum time at critical power: Once you have determined the critical power, you need to know how long you can sustain it. Tmax is the time (in seconds) that you can ride at critical power.

HIT, high-intensity interval training: These are intervals customized to your physiology. Although of short duration, they are performed at maximum effort and allow you to stress your muscles appropriately so that they become stronger.

SPAM, sustained power and muscular endurance: These intervals will specifically train the type IIa muscle fibers. During bicycle racing, you use the type IIa fibers the most.

If the lower-cadence range gave you the greatest power, you are probably using large gears. If you have trouble accelerating during races, you should train with a higher cadence or make strength training a priority.

RETESTING

There are times when repeat testing is useful as a way of monitoring your progress and training level. Here are brief comments about the three tests (refer to the "Definitions" sidebar to refresh your memory about definitions used).

Modified Conconi Testing

Performing modified Conconi testing on a regular basis is useful for determining your critical power. Because your critical power will change with training, it is a good idea to retest every 2–4 weeks during the HIT phase. The aerobic threshold heart rate and lactate threshold heart rate do not change significantly with training, so you can start the test at a power in heart rate zone 3. From there, continue to increase the power by 10 watts every minute.

If you feel you are not performing well in training and racing, you may be overtrained. Other stresses in your life—such as increased job stress, decreased sleep, or family commitments—also can contribute to being overtrained.

Repeating a Conconi test can be useful because if you fatigue sooner, this will confirm the need for increased rest. If you are overtrained and need rest, on the repeat test you will produce less power and your critical power will decrease.

Critical Power

Tracking progress with repeated critical-power testing is useful every 2–4 weeks during a HIT phase.[11] This will allow you to evaluate your time at critical power to be sure you are using the appropriate workout intensity and interval length. If you are training with power, you do not need to retest your critical power. You will know if you can increase your power as you do the intervals. If your critical power and Tmax have been improving but the improvements stop, you can move on to muscular endurance and sustained power and muscular endurance (SPAM) workouts.

To repeat the critical-power test, start with a power output that corresponds to heart rate zone 4 and continue to increase by 10 watts every minute until you reach a peak.

Repeating the modified Conconi test and critical-power test should be done on a scheduled HIT day; you can then complete the HIT training but with two fewer intervals than you normally would have completed.

Ideal Cadence

There is no need to repeat cadence testing unless you feel that your freely chosen cadence has changed significantly.

SUMMARY ■ Modified Conconi testing can show you your heart rate training zones and your peak power output.

■ Intervals are based upon percentages of the time you can maintain your peak power.

■ Training in different cadence zones will allow you to increase power without greatly increasing your work.

NOTES

1. F. Conconi, M. Ferrari, P.G. Ziglio, P. Droghetti, and L. Codeca. 1982. Determination of the anaerobic threshold by a noninvasive field test in runners. *Journal of Applied Physiology* 52, 4 (April):869–73.
F. Conconi, M. Ferrari, P.G. Ziglio, P. Droghetti, and L. Codeca. 1980. Determination of the anaerobic threshold by a noninvasive field test in man. *Bolletino della Societa Italiana di Biologia Sperimentale* 56, 23 (December 15):2504–10.

2. E. Ballarin, U. Sudhues, C. Borsetto, I. Casoni, G. Grazzi, C. Guglielmini, F. Manfredini, G. Mazzoni, and F. Conconi. 1996. Reproducibility of the Conconi test: Test repeatability and observer variations. *International Journal of Sports Medicine* 17, 7 (October):520–4.

3. B.J. Whipp and S.A. Ward. Respiratory responses of athletes to exercise. In *Oxford Textbook of Sports Medicine*, 2d ed. Oxford University Press, 1998.

4. P. Mognoni and P.E. Di Prampero. 2003. Gear, inertial work, and road slopes as determinants of biomechanics in cycling. *European Journal of Applied Physiology* 90, 3–4 (October):372–6. Epub October 7, 2003.

5. M.R. Deschenes, W.J. Kraemer, R.W. McCoy, J.S. Volek, B.M. Turner, and J.C. Weinlein. 2000. Muscle recruitment patterns regulate physiological responses during exercise of the same intensity. *American Journal of Regulatory, Integrative, and Comparative Physiology* 279, 6 (December):R2229–36.

6. J. Chavarren and J.A. Calbet. 1999. Cycling efficiency and pedalling frequency in road cyclists. *European Journal of Applied Physiology and Occupational Physiology* 80, 6 (November–December):555–63.

7. B.R. MacIntosh, R.R. Neptune, and J.F. Horton. 2000. Cadence, power, and muscle activation in cycle ergometry. *Medicine and Science in Sports and Exercise* 32, 7 (July):1281–7.

8. A. Lucia, J. Hoyos, and J.L. Chicharro. 2001. Effect of pedalling rates on physiological response during endurance cycling. *European Journal of Applied Physiology* 85, 3–4 (August):392–5.

9. D.P. Swain and J.P. Wilcox. 1992. Effect of cadence on the economy of uphill cycling. *Medicine and Science in Sports and Exercise* 24, 10 (October):1123–7.

10. R. Lepers, G.Y. Millet, N.A. Maffiuletti, C. Hausswirth, and J. Brisswalter. 2001. Effect of pedalling rates on physiological response during endurance cycling. *European Journal of Applied Physiology* 85, 3–4 (August):392–5.

11. P.B. Laursen, C.M. Shing, J.M. Peake, J.S. Coombes, and D.G. Jenkins. 2002. Interval training program optimization in highly trained endurance cyclists. *Medicine and Science in Sports and Exercise* 34, 11 (November):1801–7.

HIGH-INTENSITY TRAINING 6

I have never worked with an athlete who experienced difficulty in a race when the pace decreased. Just the opposite is true—racing becomes more difficult with increased speed. When a racer starts to have trouble, power output and heart rate are near maximum. Training at maximum intensity can be difficult, but it becomes easier when you have customized the interval intensity to match your physiology.

At maximum intensity, the muscles are relying upon all of the possible energy sources, and all types of muscle fibers are being used, which improves all areas of fitness Unfortunately, many people train only one or two of the three types of muscle fiber, leaving them gasping for air when the pace quickens.

After a sufficient period of base conditioning, a further increase in low-intensity training volume does not result in an increase in fitness.[1] Novice athletes need 10 days of increased training volume to reach the point of diminishing returns in fitness.[2] Well-trained athletes, however, do not respond to increased low-intensity endurance, but they do respond to an increase in training intensity.

The remedy for this is high-intensity training (HIT). The key to making this training intensity most effective is to know what interval lengths to use, how many to do, how to arrange them, and how to progress through a season while continuing to improve.

The increases in performance from high-intensity training are varied and significant. HIT training results in an increase in all of the following:

- Endurance capacity
- Ability to adapt to warm climates[3]
- Ability to neutralize lactic acid[4]
- Type I endurance muscle fibers[5]
- Capillaries for fatigue-resistant powerful fibers[6]
- Energy utilization[7]

INTERVAL INTENSITY

Intervals are all about hard work followed by periods of rest. The stress-recovery cycle is what leads to fitness gains. The harder you work, the better you will become, providing that you give yourself adequate recovery time. Recovery occurs between each interval and after the workout is over. Knowing how hard to work can be tricky. If you have tested your critical power as outlined in Chapter 5, you have already determined your target intensity.

As you increase exercise intensity from rest, you start to add different muscle fibers. All three muscle-fiber types are being used at 85–100% of critical power. Beyond this intensity, increases in effort will not result in further oxygen utilization by the body because the effort is already near maximal.

The hallmark for endurance athletes is the VO_2max. To date, VO_2max measurement is not readily available to most athletes. critical power derived from a Conconi test (Chapter 5), however, yields the same information. At critical power, each of the muscle-fiber types benefits from the training effect. Once you know the maximum power, you can determine interval length.

INTERVAL LENGTH

The appropriate duration of an interval is highly variable and depends upon your physiology. Weight lifting offers an example. If you are lifting a weight for 15 repetitions but can fully complete only 12 of those repetitions, the last 3 repetitions you struggle through are not of any significant training value. Likewise, if you set out to perform a 3-minute interval in cycling but are performing adequately for only 1 minute, the next 2 minutes are not helping your performance and are only shortening your recovery. To avoid this fruitless effort, you need to determine the interval length that will work best for you.

Interval lengths are personal and should be less than the maximum time to fatigue at critical power. After establishing critical power through a modified Conconi test (Chapter 5), record the time that you can sustain critical power. The maximum time for sustained critical power is abbreviated as Tmax. (Refer to Chapter 5 for descriptions of the critical power and modified Conconi tests). Tmax usually ranges from 50 seconds to 2 minutes.

At critical power, most athletes need at least 50% or 60% of the Tmax to reach maximum training effect.[8] Table 6.1 illustrates a variety of HIT workouts with proven results.

RECOVERY

Lactic acid is generated during the highly anaerobic HIT workouts and contributes to muscle fatigue. Lactic acid is best removed from the muscles through active recovery. A 20-minute, high-cadence, low-resistance cool-down can remove lactic acid.

After HIT, there is significant fatigue or injury to the muscle fibers. Providing adequate recovery, both between intervals and at the end of a workout, allows the muscles to heal and repair. After HIT workouts, the changes during recovery lead to increased strength, but if your recovery is inadequate, the exercise-induced changes lead to overtraining (see Figure 6.1).

TABLE 6.1 High-intensity interval training (HIT) workouts

REPS	VOLUME (% of critical power)	INTENSITY	RECOVERY	IMPROVEMENTS
8	60% Tmax	100	1:2 ratio of work: rest	40km time trial[1]
8	60% Tmax	100	65% max HR	40km time trial[2]
12	30 sec	175	4.5 min	Cycling performance[3]
20	60 sec	100	120 sec	4 sessions over 2 weeks resulted in increased critical power[4]
120	15 sec	100	15 sec	More fat used as fuel, less glycogen used[5]
5	4 min	100	2 min	Increased oxidative capacity of Type II muscle fibers[6]
8	4 min	85	1 min	Improved critical power[7]
6-8	5 min	80	1 min	Absolute and relative power output[8]
6-8	5 min	80	1 min	6 sessions in 4 weeks improved lactic acid buffering capacity and endurance performance[9]
6-9	5 min	80	1 min	2 sessions/week for 12 weeks sustain higher percentages of peak power in 40km time-trial performance[10]
8	5 min	86	1 min	Increased carbohydrate and fat oxidation[11]
6-8	5 min	80	1 min	4-week program increased PPO and fatigue resistance and improved 40km time trial[12]

TABLE 6.1, continued

NOTES:

1. P.B. Laursen, C.M. Shing, J.M. Peake, J.S. Coombes, and D.G. Jenkins. 2002. Interval training program optimization in highly trained endurance cyclists. *Medicine and Science in Sports and Exercise* 34, 11 (November):1801-7.

2. Laursen et al. November 2002.

3. Laursen et al. November 2002.

4. P.B. Laursen, M.A. Blanchard, and D.G. Jenkins. 2002. Acute high-intensity interval training improves Tvent and peak power output in highly trained males. *Canadian Journal of Applied Physiology* 27, 4 (August):336-48.

5. B. Essen, L. Hagenfeldt, and L. Kaijser. 1977. Utilization of blood-borne and intramuscular substrates during continuous and intermittent exercise in man. *Journal of Physiology* 265 (1977): 489-506.

6. L.V. Billat. 2001. Interval training for performance: A scientific and empirical practice. Part II: Anaerobic interval training. Sports Medicine 31, 2 (February):75-90.

7. Billat 2001.

8. F.H. Lindsay, J.A. Hawley, K.H. Myburgh, H.H. Schomer, T.D. Noakes, and S.C. Dennis. 1996. Improved athletic performance in highly trained cyclists after interval training. Medicine and Science in Sports and Exercise 28, 11 (November):1427-34.

9. A.R. Weston, K.H. Myburgh, F.H. Lindsay, S.C. Dennis, T.D. Noakes, and J.A. Hawley. 1997. Skeletal muscle buffering capacity and endurance performance after high-intensity interval training by well-trained cyclists. European Journal of Appllied Physiology and Occupational Physiology. 75(1):7-13.

10. C. Westgarth-Taylor, J.A. Hawley, S. Rickard, K.H. Myburgh, T.D. Noakes, and S.C. Dennis. 1997. Metabolic and performance adaptations to interval training in endurance-trained cyclists. European Journal of Applied Physiology and Occupational Physiology 75 (4):298-304.

11. N.K.Stepto, D.T. Martin, K.E. Fallon, et al. 2001. Metabolic demands of intense aerobic interval training in competitive cyclists. Medicine and Science in Sports and Exercise 33 (2001): 303-10.

12. Lindsay et al. November 1996.

HIT not only works the muscles but trains them to recover as well. Short recovery (1 minute) HIT protocols provide more stress and better lactic-acid buffering compared with a longer recovery HIT program.[9] If a shorter recovery period is used, however, you will become fatigued sooner and will complete fewer work intervals. Fewer work intervals mean decreased improvement. The length of recovery should depend upon each athlete's experience. The longer end of the recovery range should be chosen for those who are new to interval training. If you are new

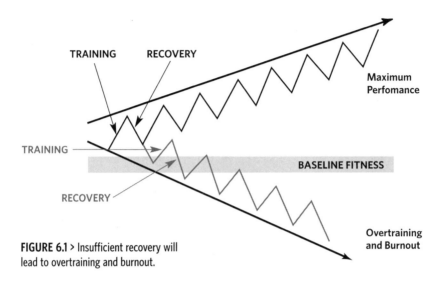

FIGURE 6.1 > Insufficient recovery will lead to overtraining and burnout.

to HIT, you should allow your heart rate to decrease below the aerobic threshold, or you should allow 2 minutes for a recovery interval (Table 6.2). Those with interval experience or who have completed 2–4 weeks of HIT can choose a shorter recovery interval.

TABLE 6.2 HIT recovery protocols

SHORT RECOVERY
30 seconds
1 minute

LONG RECOVERY
Twice the length of the work interval
2 minutes
Heart rate to 65% of maximum

WORKOUTS IN THE REAL WORLD: FROM THE LAB TO YOU

High-intensity interval training uses shorter intervals than are traditionally used. The short, maximal intervals can lead to improvements more quickly than can typical interval training at the lactate threshold heart rate.[10]

To avoid getting stale, you should use intervals of different lengths. When your power stops increasing, switch to longer intervals.

Planning Workouts

There are a few considerations when combining HIT workouts to develop a training program. Because of the intense nature of exercise, the workout days and the recovery days should be grouped to allow for maximum recovery. This schedule provides an intense training stimulus followed by a generous recovery period. This can be done as 4 days in a row of training followed by 3 days off. Similarly, 3 on and 3 off can be done, but this schedule does not fit as well into the calendar week. Individuals who can recover well can do 5 days on and 2 off, but in general I do not recommend this schedule.

The calendar week might look something like this:

	Plan 1	Plan 2	Plan 3
Saturday	HIT	HIT	HIT
Sunday	HIT	HIT	HIT
Monday	HIT	HIT	HIT
Tuesday	off	off	HIT
Wednesday	off	off	off
Thursday	off	off	off
Friday	off	HIT	off

When you first move from weight training and endurance building, it is a good idea to start with plan 1. If that is well tolerated for a week and you are able to perform the HIT workouts the following week, you can adopt a schedule more like plan 2. The problem with this plan is that you will always be starting your workouts on a different day of the week. Schedule the days before the weekend as days off. This works well if there is a race for the weekend, but if you choose plan 2, there will be a week where you will not have the three days off prior to the weekend and you may approach a race with more or less rest time than you would like. To regulate the schedule well, I like to progress to plan 3. This gives you fixed days for training and rest.

In the many research studies with HIT, there were up to 6 weekly HIT sessions, but most used 2–4 sessions a week. If you find that performing intervals on day 3 or 4 is too difficult, you can alternate HIT days with other workouts and progressively add days of HIT training. Performing the HIT workouts on alternating days ensures adequate time for the muscle-building actions of the body to repair any damage to the muscles that have been stressed. Maintain the recovery block. Those 3 days of rest will allow the body to recover from overreaching and most overtraining. If you are not recovering from repeated HIT workouts as described above, try arranging your week like this:

	Plan 1	Plan 2
Saturday	HIT	HIT
Sunday	HIT	Endurance
Monday	Endurance	HIT
Tuesday	off	Endurance
Wednesday	off	off
Thursday	off	off
Friday	HIT	off

Using power or speed is the best way to track your performance with HIT workouts. Because of the intense nature of the exercise and the relatively short interval length, heart rate is not very useful, as the heart rate might not be elevated to the desired level until after the interval is over.

The goal with HIT is to be able to sustain longer periods at intensity and increase both critical power and power at lactate threshold. To monitor progress, you need to get your power to the appropriate level as quickly as possible after the interval starts. If you do not train with power, speed can be used if the road on which you are training is a constant grade with a constant wind speed and direction.

One reason to use HIT is to train at your maximum for a longer total time than if you were training with longer intervals.[11] While 15- and 30-second intervals have been shown to work well for many athletes,[12] interval length should also be chosen so that it is specific to your physiology.

If you have tested your critical power, you must then test how long you can sustain that intensity (Tmax). Interval length is a percentage of Tmax. You should use 50%, 60%, and 70% of Tmax as interval lengths.

Structuring Workouts: Daily Undulating Periodization

Once you have determined the 50–70% of Tmax for intervals, you can start to arrange these interval lengths in a way that maximizes the training effect. Regardless of whether you are using power or speed to track the work intensity, it is important to know at what level you are training. If you only want to increase low-intensity endurance, you would increase interval length while decreasing interval intensity.[13] Rotating through increasingly more difficult exercises every day on a weekly basis develops muscular strength along with endurance.[14]

The process of changing work volume on a daily basis is called *daily undulating periodization*. Traditionally, trainers increase intensity one day at a time, and athletes' efforts get harder only day-to-day and week-to-week. With daily undulating periodization, difficulty will progress throughout the week, then become easier at the start of the next week. Daily undulating periodization will build strength faster.

Because the intensity will be the same every day (near maximal effort), intervals can be made more difficult by increasing the time at critical power. Applying the daily undulating periodization for two weeks might produce this schedule:

	Interval Length	Intensity
Saturday	50% Tmax	Critical Power
Sunday	60% Tmax	Critical Power
Monday	70% Tmax	Critical Power
Tuesday	off	
Wednesday	off	
Thursday	off	
Friday	50% Tmax	Critical Power + 10 watts
Saturday	60% Tmax	Critical Power + 10 watts
Sunday	70% Tmax	Critical Power + 10 watts

Throughout the training week, you are working harder each day with intervals at 50%, 60%, and 70% of Tmax. At the start of the next training week, the 50% Tmax interval will seem short in comparison with the previous week, and you should feel as though you can increase the interval intensity. With time, you should be able to sustain more power over longer intervals.

Increases in power and strength are not indefinite, however. Eventually the increases in power output will stop. This will likely happen after 4 to 6 weeks of HIT, but may occur in as little as 2 weeks.

After the increases in power output start to plateau, it is time to move toward increased muscular endurance.

SUSTAINED POWER (MUSCULAR ENDURANCE) INTERVALS

Once you have become comfortable exercising for brief periods at near maximal intensity, the intervals can be lengthened and the intensity decreased.

By decreased intensity, I am not implying that the heart rate should be low. On the contrary, the intervals should still be at a high intensity, but they are not at critical power. Instead, a range of 80–85% of the critical power should be used.[15] At this power intensity, the interval length can be up to 5 minutes.

Start with shorter intervals (4 minutes) with longer rest periods (2 minutes). When you are able to complete these workouts without a drop in power, move on to shorter recovery times (1 minute). If you are able to do these workouts without a drop in power, then you can increase the interval length (5 minutes). When you increase the interval length from 4 to 5 minutes, increase the recovery time from 1 minute to 2 minutes. When you can easily perform work at 80–85% of critical power, shorten the recovery time before increasing the interval length. Refer to Table 6.1 for examples of these workouts.

You will notice that the interval lengths are 4 and 5 minutes. Once you have progressed through 8 or 9 of the 5-minute intervals at 80-85% critical power with a 1-minute recovery, it is time to reassess your critical power. Since it is undoubtedly higher after training, you should begin the cycle again starting with 4-minute intervals and 2 minutes of rest, but at 80% of your new critical power.

Despite the temptation to do so, you do not want to increase your interval length beyond 5 minutes. The type IIa muscle fibers become fatigued and do not work well beyond 4–5 minutes. Once this happens, recovery will be prolonged. If you can hold your power beyond the 4–5 minute interval periods, try these intervals with a power that is 10 watts higher. Increase power as needed to give yourself intervals that you can do for 4 to 5 minutes.

Sustained power and muscular endurance (SPAM) intervals should be done twice in a 4-day training block, alternated with HIT intervals at critical power. Once you have been doing HIT intervals for 2 week, you can add Sustained Power workouts. A sample schedule might look like this:

Saturday	HIT
Sunday	SPAM
Monday	HIT
Tuesday	SPAM
Wednesday	off
Thursday	off
Friday	off

It was once believed that you had to stress your body to the point of complete fatigue to make strength gains. In fact, failure is not needed to increase strength.[16] Instead of pushing your body to the point of fatigue, you should work harder for a shorter period of time. The type IIa muscle fibers will not support work for more than a few minutes, and working longer will not provide any benefit.

The reason you have gone through all of the work in testing yourself is to find interval lengths that will best allow your muscles to adapt to the demands of training. I like to use the analogy of push-ups. If you are doing push-ups and get your chest down to the floor on the first six, but are barely able to lift up your body after that, it is time to stop. If you continue but are still counting, you are not really doing any more push-ups. The same is true if your power output falls off during a cycling interval: You may still be turning the pedals, but you are not enhancing the training effect.

EXPLOSIVE POWER

Developing explosive power is important for sprinting, attacking, jumping out of corners, and getting over short, steep hills. Training for explosive power will also help with endurance over short distances.[17] One method of attaining explosive power is through the use of *postactivation potentiation*, or PAP.

Postactivation potentiation (PAP) occurs when an extremely hard muscle effort makes subsequent efforts easier. First a maximal contraction is done for

10 seconds, then the next contraction effort is faster and stronger. This results in a faster, more forceful contraction with the same perceived effort. To experience PAP for yourself, try this exercise. Lift your right arm out to the side as fast as you can. Now repeat the same motion, only this time, stand with your right side against a wall and try to raise your right arm out to the side. Press against the wall as hard as you can for 10 seconds. Now step away from the wall and lift your arm to the side as before. It should feel as though it wants to rise up by itself (Photo 6.1).

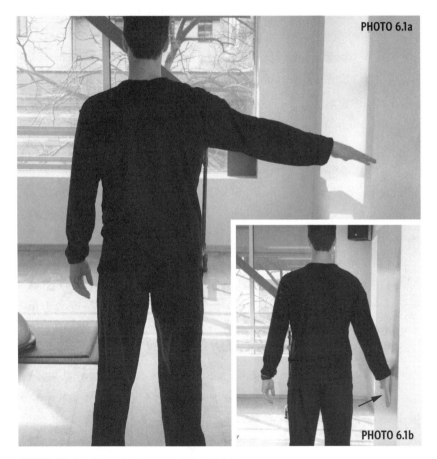

PHOTO 6.1a/b > Postactivation potentiation of right arm

In this instance, the maximal isometric contraction (pushing against the wall as hard as you can) primes the muscles to work harder and faster the second time. PAP has been shown to be useful in both endurance and explosive-sport athletes.[18] Unlike fatigue, where previous contractions impair performance, PAP relies on previous contractions to improve performance.

The types of exercises that will benefit most from PAP are well defined. PAP is more prevalent in the faster, more powerful type IIb muscle fibers, making it more useful for developing short, powerful contractions, as in sprinting.[19]

PAP is useful in training short efforts at high intensity. Increasing sprint performance requires training type IIb fibers. Activation of these fibers starts at 80–85% of critical power, but they are not fully recruited until you are training at your absolute maximum power. You can use 175% of critical power (1.75 x critical power) as intensity with increased performance. Remember, critical power is the peak power you achieved during the modified Conconi test; it is not the maximum power you can generate.

The effect of the near maximal isometric contraction has been recognized, but you need to determine the length of recovery time between the maximal contraction and the start of the work interval. Although it is accepted that the rest interval should be between 15 seconds and 3 minutes, this is still a large range.[20]

Some experimentation is needed, but here's how to use PAP. First, sprint on a level road and take note of the power you produced. This is the *index sprint*. Next, find a hill that levels out at the top. The hill should be steep enough that when using a large gear, you are barely able to turn the pedals.

When you are ready to begin the interval, you will shift into a large gear and head up the hill, this is the *maximal contraction*. Pedal at this high load and low cadence for 20 seconds.[21] After you finish the heavy-load exercise, you should be at the top of the hill (Figure 6.2). Shift into a smaller gear and pedal easily for 15 seconds before sprinting. The power and speed you produced should be higher than the index sprint. If the power and speed were lower than the index

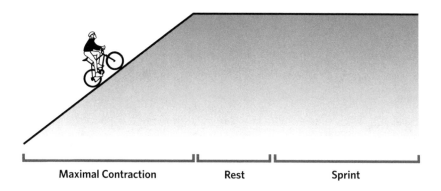

| Maximal Contraction | Rest | Sprint |

FIGURE 6.2 > Postactivation potentiation: After a 20-second maximal contraction riding uphill in a large gear, rest for 15 seconds, then begin your sprint interval. The maximal contraction with low cadence will make the muscles work harder during the sprint.

sprint, you need to incorporate longer rest periods between the heavy-load interval and the sprint interval. Try rest periods of 30 seconds, 60 seconds, 2 minutes, and 3 minutes to see which one results in increased sprinting power.

TRAINING CONSIDERATIONS

Training is not just about hard work; it is also about recovery. If you work hard but don't recover, you will not improve. Because interval training is physically demanding, you must ensure that your body is ready for the hard work.

Nutritional Concerns in Interval Training

HIT presents two significant nutritional concerns. First, iron stores have been shown to decrease over six weeks of HIT training.[22] This can have an adverse effect on performance, as it will lead to a decrease in the oxygen-delivering capacity of the blood.[23] Without oxygen, your body will not be as efficient in generating energy. I recommend a daily multivitamin with iron during the HIT phase. Taking iron after a workout can increase absorption.[24]

Second, glycogen is metabolized at a high rate during interval training.[25] Thus you must be vigilant about replacing glycogen after exercise with a meal of 1 gram of carbohydrate and 0.3 grams of protein per kilogram of body weight (.5 gram of carbohydrate and .15 gram of protein per pound of body weight). This is most easily accomplished as a liquid meal and is better tolerated if it is sweet and cool. Have one meal immediately after exercise and another one hour after exercise. See Chapter 11 for recipes for smoothies and appropriate meals.

Temporal Specificity

Research also has shown that HIT is specific to the time of day you train. In other words, if you do all of your training in the morning but race in the afternoon, you might not get all of the effects of HIT that you should.[26] If possible, schedule one of your HIT sessions at a time when you would normally be racing.

Training just above the type IIa level will induce the training effect in type I and IIa muscle fibers. In addition, working at short, intense intervals will prevent fatigue in the muscles and allow for more time at or near your maximum.[27] Working harder for longer will increase your maximum power, time-trial performance, buffering of lactic acid, and the ability of the muscles to use oxygen as a fuel. In sum, the rationale for performing high-intensity intervals is real and proven.

SUMMARY ■ High-intensity interval training recruits all of your muscle fibers.

■ Only muscle fibers that are recruited will benefit from training.

■ High-intensity intervals are calculated based upon your critical power and the time you can sustain critical power.

■ Using daily undulating periodization will maximize training work.

■ Sprinting power can be developed with the concept of postactivation potentiation.

■ Sustained power and muscular endurance is best trained at 80–85% of critical power.

■ Maintaining adequate carbohydrate and iron stores is important to the success of HIT workouts.

NOTES

1. B.R. Londeree. 1997. Effect of training on lactate/ventilatory thresholds: A meta-analysis. *Medicine and Science in Sports and Exercise* 29,6 (June):837–43.

2. H.J. Green, L.L. Jones, and D.C. Painter. 1990. Effects of short-term training on cardiac function during prolonged exercise. *Medicine and Science in Sports and Exercise* 22, 4 (August):488–93.

H.J. Green, G. Coates, J.R. Sutton, et al. 1991. Early adaptations in gas exchange, cardiac function, and haematology to prolonged exercise training in man. *European Journal of Applied Physiology and Occupational Physiology* 63, 1 (January):17–23.

H.J. Green, S. Jones, M. Ball-Burnett, et al. 1991. Early adaptations in blood substrates, metabolites, and hormones to prolonged exercise training in man. *Canadian Journal of Physiology and Pharmacology* 69, 8 (August):1222–9.

S.M. Phillips, H.J. Green, M.A. Tarnopolsky, et al. 1996. Progressive effect of endurance training on metabolic adaptations in working skeletal muscle. *American Journal of Physiology* 270, 2 Pt 1 (February):E265–72.

S.M. Phillips, H.J. Green, M.A. Tarnopolsky, et al. 1996. Effects of training duration on substrate turnover and oxidation during exercise. *Journal of Applied Physiology* 81, 5 (November):2182–91.

3. L.E. Armstrong and C.M. Maresh. 1998. Effects of training, environment, and hot factors on the sweating response to exercise. *International Journal of Sports Medicine* 19, Supp. 2 (June): S103–5.

4. P.B. Laursen and D.G. Jenkins. 2002. The scientific basis for high-intensity interval training: Optimising training programmes and maximising performance in highly trained endurance athletes. *Sports Medicine* 32 (1):53–73.

5. M.T. Linossier, C. Dennis, D. Dormois, et al. 1993. Ergometric and metabolic adaptation to a 5-s sprint training programme. *European Journal of Applied Physiology and Occupational Physiology* 67, 5 (1993): 408–14.

6. D. Bishop, D.G. Jenkins, M. McEniery, et al. 2000. Relationship between plasma lactate parameters and muscle characteristics in female cyclists. *Medicine and Science in Sports and Exercise* 32, 6 (June): 1088–93.

7. G. Rodas, J.L. Ventura, J.A. Cadefau, et al. 2000. A short training programme for the rapid improvement of both aerobic and anaerobic metabolism. *European Journal of Applied Physiology* 82, 5-6 (August):480–6.

J. Parra, J.A. Cadefau, G. Rodas, et al. 2000. The distribution of rest periods affects performance and adaptations of energy metabolism induced by high-intensity training in human muscle. *Acta Physiologica Scandinavia* 169,2 (June): 157–65.

J.D. MacDougall, A.L. Hicks, J.R. MacDonald, et al. 1998. Muscle performance and enzymatic adaptations to sprint interval training. *Journal of Applied Physiology* 84, 6 (June):2138–42.

M.T. Linossier, C. Dennis, D. Dormois, et al. 1993.

8. D.W. Hill and A.L. Rowell. 1997. Responses to exercise at the velocity associated with VO_2max. *Medicine and Science in Sports and Exercise* 29,1 (January):113–6.

V.L. Billat, B. Flechet, B. Petit, G. Muriaux, and J.P. Koralsztein. 1999. Interval training at VO_2max: Effects on aerobic performance and overtraining markers. *Medicine and Science in Sports and Exercise* 31, 1 (January):156–63.

9. P.D. Balsom, J.Y. Seger, B. Sjodin, et al. 1992. Maximal-intensity intermittent exercise: Effect of recovery duration. *International Journal of Sports Medicine* 13, 7 (October):528–33.

10. S.R. Norris and S.R. Petersen. 1998. Effects of endurance training on transient oxygen uptake responses in cyclists. *Journal of Sports Sciences* 16, 8 (November):733–8.

F.H. Lindsay, J.A. Hawley, K.H. Myburgh, H.H. Schomer, T.D. Noakes, and S.C. Dennis. 1996. Improved athletic performance in highly trained cyclists after interval training. *Medicine and Science in Sports and Exercise* 28, 11 (November):1427–34.

11. V.L. Billat, J. Slawinksi, V. Bocquet, P. Chassaing, A. Demarle, and J.P. Koralsztein. 2001. Very short (15s–15s) interval-training around the critical velocity allows middle-aged runners to maintain VO_2max for 14 minutes. *International Journal of Sports Medicine* 22, 3 (April):201–8.

12. Billat et al. 2001.

13. M.R. Rhea, W.T. Phillips, L.N. Burkett, W.J. Stone, S.D. Ball, B.A. Alvar, and A.B. Thomas. 2003. A comparison of linear and daily undulating periodized programs with equated volume and intensity for local muscular endurance. *Journal of Strength and Conditioning Research* 17, 1 (February):82–7.

14. M.R. Rhea, S.D. Ball, W.T. Phillips, and L.N. Burkett. 2002. A comparison of linear and daily undulating periodized programs with equated volume and intensity for strength. *Journal of Strength and Conditioning Research* 16, 2 (May):250–5.

15. A.R. Weston, K.H. Myburgh, F.H. Lindsay, S.C. Dennis, T.D. Noakes, and J.A. Hawley. 1997. Skeletal muscle buffering capacity and endurance performance after high-intensity interval training by well-trained cyclists. *European Journal of Applied Physiology and Occupational Physiology* 75 (1):7–13.

C. Westgarth-Taylor, J.A. Hawley, S. Rickard, K.H. Myburgh, T.D. Noakes, and S.C. Dennis. 1997. Metabolic and performance adaptations to interval training in endurance-trained cyclists. *European Journal of Applied Physiology and Occupational Physiology* 75 (4):298–304.

N.K. Stepto, D.T. Martin, K.E. Fallon, et al. 2001. Metabolic demands of intense aerobic interval training in competitive cyclists. *Medicine and Science in Sports and Exercise* 33, 2 (February):303–10.

16. J.P. Folland, C.S. Irish, J.C. Roberts, J.E. Tarr, and D.A. Jones. 2002. Fatigue is not a necessary stimulus for strength gains during resistance training. *British Journal of Sports Medicine* 36, 5 (October):370–3.

S. Katsuta, Y. Kanao, and Y. Aoyagi. 1988. Is exhaustive training adequate preparation for endurance performance? *European Journal of Applied Physiology and Occupational Physiology* 58 (1–2):68–73.

17. L. Paavolainen, K. Hakkinen, I. Hamalainen, A. Nummela, and H. Rusko. 1999. Explosive-strength training improves 5-km running time by improving running economy and muscle power. *Journal of Applied Physiology* 86, 5 (May):1527–33.

18. L.Z. Chiu, A.C. Fry, L.W. Weiss, B.K. Schilling, L.E. Brown, and S.L. Smith. 2003. Postactivation potentiation response in athletic and recreationally trained individuals. *Journal of Strength and Conditioning Research* 17, 4 (November):671–7.

T. Hamada, D.G. Sale, and J.D. MacDougall. 2000. Postactivation potentiation in endurance-trained male athletes. *Medicine and Science in Sports and Exercise* 32, 2 (February):403–11.

19. T. Hamada, D.G. Sale, J.D. MacDougall, and M.A. Tarnopolsky. 2000. Postactivation potentiation, fiber type, and twitch contraction time in human knee extensor muscles. *Journal of Applied Physiology* 88, 6 (June):2131–7.

20 E.R. Gossen and D.G. Sale. 2000. Effect of postactivation potentiation on dynamic knee extension performance. *European Journal of Applied Physiology* 83, 6 (June):524–30.

D.G. Sale. 2002. Postactivation potentiation: Role in human performance. *Exercise and Sport Sciences Reviews* 30, 3 (July):138–43.

21. D.N. French, W.J. Kraemer, and C.B. Cooke. 2003. Changes in dynamic exercise performance following a sequence of preconditioning isometric muscle actions. *Journal of Strength and Conditioning Research* 17, 4 (November):678–85.

22. J.G. Wilkinson, D.T. Martin, A.A. Adams, and M. Liebman. 2002. Iron status in cyclists during high-intensity interval training and recovery. *International Journal of Sports Medicine* 23, 8 (November):544–8.

23. M.V. Perkkio, L.T. Jansson, G.A. Brooks, C.J. Refino, and P.R. Dallman. 1985. Work performance in iron deficiency of increasing severity. *Journal of Applied Physiology* 58, 5 (May):1477–80.

24. A. Schmid, E. Jakob, A. Berg, T. Russmann, D. Konig, M. Irmer, and J. Keul. 1996. Effect of physical exercise and vitamin C on absorption of ferric sodium citrate. *Medicine and Science in Sports and Exercise* 28, 12 (December):1470–3.

25. N.K. Stepto, D.T. Martin, K.E. Fallon, and J.A. Hawley. 2001. Metabolic demands of intense aerobic interval training in competitive cyclists. *Medicine and Science in Sports and Exercise* 33, 2 (February):303–10.

26. D.W. Hill, J.A. Leiferman, N.A. Lynch, B.S. Dangelmaier, and S.E. Burt. 1998. Temporal specificity in adaptations to high-intensity exercise training. *Medicine and Science in Sports and Exercise* 30, 3 (March):450–5.

27. Billat et al. 2001.

RESISTANCE TRAINING 7

Endurance athletes and strength athletes have traditionally been in two separate camps in terms of training. Strength and power athletes (lifters, football and baseball players) would avoid doing any endurance training, and it was equally unlikely that the endurance athletes would be found in the weight room.

One myth held that resistance training would cause a large increase in muscle mass that would slow a cyclist on the hills. Resistance training, however, can increase power and endurance capacity, improve recovery, and prevent loss of fitness.

Resistance training can increase power and endurance capacity, improve recovery, and prevent loss of fitness.

Using force to enhance muscle development has been called many things. Weight training implies the use of iron plates and resistance machines. I prefer the term *resistance training* because sometimes only body weight is used to provide resistance.

No matter the name, the benefits of this approach are clear. An increase in your maximum power can be expected with resistance training.[1] The resistance-trained athlete can maintain fitness for longer periods of time off the bicycle. Increased recovery results in the ability to go harder at the next training session, which increases fitness.[2]

Like interval training, resistance training brings an increase in type IIa muscle fibers.[3] As discussed in Chapter 3, the IIa fibers will help in cycling. Resistance training will induce growth of all of the muscle fibers and increase the endurance capacity.[4] In contrast, prolonged endurance training can decrease the peak power and size of the muscle fibers.[5] The increased endurance capacity from resistance training may come from increased muscle efficiency.[6]

Resistance training should be used in combination with endurance training to achieve maximum benefit. During resistance training the muscles grow without an increase in mitochondria or capillaries. This is like increasing the size of the factory without bringing in new supplies or new factory workers. The help that the cells have is diluted. By combining specific endurance and strength workouts, you can increase strength, increase mitochondria, and promote capillary growth.[7]

PRINCIPLES OF RESISTANCE TRAINING
Volume

Resistance training is broken down into sets and repetitions. A *set* is the period of exercise that is separated from the next set by a rest period. The number of *repetitions* is the number of times you move the weight in each set.

One long-held belief about resistance training is that the muscles had to be worked to the point of fatigue for increases in strength to take place. This now has been discounted.[8] Although you want to lift as much as you can for the prescribed number of repetitions, you do not have to perform repeated sets until you can no longer lift the weight. When you are doing an 8 repetition maximum (8RM, or 8 rep max), you should be using the most weight you can manage for 8 repetitions. If you are unable to do 8 reps, then you must use less

TABLE 7.1 Matching weight to repetitions

IF YOU CAN DO	INCREASE WEIGHT BY
1 or 2 reps more	5 lbs
3 or 4 reps more	10 lbs
5 or 6 reps more	15 lbs

IF YOU FALL SHORT BY	DECREASE WEIGHT BY
1 or 2 reps	5 lbs
3 or 4 reps	10 lbs
5 or 6 reps	15 lbs

weight; if you are able to do more reps, you need to increase the weight. To adjust weight for the number of repetitions, see Table 7.1.

The number of reps is manipulated depending upon the effect you are trying to achieve (Figure 7.1). Between 2 and 6 repetitions, you are building strength; between 8 and 12 repetitions, you are increasing the muscle-fiber size.[9] Above 15 repetitions, you are building muscular endurance, which is probably best done on the bicycle to maintain sport-specific training.

REPETITIONS 1 - 2 - 3 - 4 - 5 - 6 - 7 - 8 - 9 - 10 - 11 - 12 - 13 - 14 - 15 - 16 - 17 - 18 - 19 - 20

GOAL   Strength   Hypertrophy   Muscular Endurance

1-6	Repetitions will build strength
8-12	Repetitions will increase the size of the muscles
15-20	Repetitions build endurance

FIGURE 7.1 > Using different repetitions to meet your goals

Strength gains can be made with 2 or 3 days of lifting a week. Lifting 2 days will provide you with only 80% of the gains that you might see in 3 days.[10]

The supplement creatine has gained popularity among proponents of weight training; to determine suitability of creatine supplementation for building strength, consult the sidebar "Should I use creatine?".

Should I use creatine?

Creatine is a protein that is found naturally in muscle. Creatine binds with phosphate to create a high-energy compound that is used for brief, very high-intensity exercise. In the same way that carbohydrate can fuel intensity and short-term exercise, an increase in the phosphocreatine pool can help to fuel high-intensity strength and sprint exercise. It is most valuable for athletes looking to increase strength and muscle mass.

To increase phosphocreatine stores in the muscle with the fewest side effects, take a daily dose of 3mg (5mg for vegetarians). Your body will need approximately four weeks to reach the necessary levels.[1] If you are going to use creatine, plan to start supplementing to coincide with the hypertrophy phase. Also plan on spending six weeks in the hypertrophy phase, doing high reps with increasing weight throughout the phase.

Creatine is not for use for those with kidney disease. Also, it is important to stay well hydrated and consume a high-carbohydrate meal with creatine to help with absorption.[2] Because the side effects are detrimental to the endurance athlete, keep them to a minimum by using a four-week loading phase.

NOTES:

1. E. Hultman, K. Soderlund, J.A. Timmons, G. Cederblad, and P.L. Greenhaff. 1996. Muscle creatine loading in men. *Journal of Applied Physiology* 81, 1 (July):232–7.

2. A.L. Green, E. Hultman, I.A. Macdonald, D.A. Sewell, and P.L. Greenhaff. 1996. Carbohydrate ingestion augments skeletal muscle creatine accumulation during creatine supplementation in humans. *American Journal of Physiology, Endocrinology, and Metabolism* 271, 5 Pt 1 (November):E821–6.

Specificity

Sport-specific training, or *specificity*, is important to consider when you are doing resistance training. Because you are not on the bicycle, the movements should be as close to cycling movements as possible. Specificity in position, warm-up, and speed of movements is important in resistance training.

Specificity can be aided by incorporating sport-specific activity into your resistance-training workout, such as warming up on a trainer or riding a bicycle to the gym.[11] The position you take during weight training is also important.[12] When you perform exercises such as squats or leg presses, keep your feet parallel and as wide as they would be on a bicycle.

A common belief is that turning your feet out or keeping a wide stance will increase the muscular benefits, but it is important to maintain a posture that most closely re-sembles the cycling position. Similarly, it is

Specificity in position, warm-up, and speed of movements is important in resistance training.

probably not necessary to bend your knees completely when you perform squats, since your knees are never bent that much when you are riding.

Speed of movement during resistance training should also be specific. Faster resistance training increases muscular force, increases fast-twitch muscle fibers, and leads to increased maximal strength.[13] Velocity-specific resistance training tends to increase strength at the velocity at which you are training.[14]

Types of movements

During each repetition of an exercise, the weight is raised (the muscle contracts as it works) and lowered (the muscle is lengthened under force). Raising the weight is called concentric movement; lowering the weight is called eccentric movement. This chapter focuses primarily on concentric/eccentric lifting. There is also isometric resistance, in which the muscle length does not change with force. An example of isometric movement is pushing against a stationary object, similar to the maximal contraction in PAP.

The concentric phase will help you move the weight, but the eccentric phase is what makes you improve. The eccentric phase places stress on the muscle, which after recovery causes increased strength. During eccentric movements, the structural fibers of the tendons are better aligned, resulting in stronger tendons. When you are doing resistance training, the eccentric phase should be slow and controlled. If you follow this simple piece of advice, you will have increased strength and stronger tendons.

Delayed-onset muscle soreness (DOMS)

Delayed-onset muscle soreness (DOMS) is all too familiar for the elite and novice athlete alike. DOMS results from intense exercise to which the athlete is unaccustomed, especially at the beginning of the season after some time away from training. Although it appears to result more from eccentric movements (lowering weight), the exact cause of DOMS is unknown. Without question, however, the soreness can be debilitating and can lead to a decrease in peak strength, an increase in perceived exertion, and pain with movement.

Anti-inflammatory medications such as ibuprofen (400mg every 8 hours, started 4 hours before exercise) and vitamin C (200mg twice daily for 2 weeks before starting exercise) can help to decrease the pain and soreness. The role of massage is less well known but appears to have some positive effects on recovery.

Exercise is the most effective modality for decreasing pain from DOMS, but the effect is temporary. Most DOMS will resolve spontaneously within 2–3 days after exercise.

REFERENCES:

K. Cheung, P. Hume, and L. Maxwell. 2003. Delayed onset muscle soreness: Treatment strategies and performance factors. *Sports Medicine* 33, 2 (2003):145-64.

T. Farr, C. Nottle, K. Nosaka, and P. Sacco. 2002. The effects of therapeutic massage on delayed onset muscle soreness and muscle function following downhill walking. *Journal of Science and Medicine in Sport/Sports Medicine Australia.* 5, 4 (December):297-306.

J.E. Hilbert, G.A. Sforzo, and T. Swensen. 2003. The effects of massage on delayed onset muscle soreness. *British Journal of Sports Medicine* 37, 1 (February):72-5.

K.E. Scott, R. Rozenek, A.C. Russo, J.A. Crussemeyer, and M.G. Lacourse. 2003. Effects of delayed onset muscle soreness on selected physiological responses to submaximal running. *Journal of Strength and Conditioning Research* 17, 4 (November):652-8.

D. Thompson, C. Williams, S. J. McGregor, C.W. Nicholas, F. McArdle, M.J. Jackson, and J.R. Powell. 2001. Prolonged vitamin C supplementation and recovery from demanding exercise. *International Journal of Sport Nutrition and Exercise Metabolism* 11, 4 (December):466-81.

S.P. Tokmakidis, E.A. Kokkinidis, I. Smilios, and H. Douda. 2003. The effects of ibuprofen on delayed muscle soreness and muscular performance after eccentric exercise. *Journal of Strength and Conditioning Research* 17, 1 (February):53-9.

If you climb with a low cadence and lift with low speed, your strength gains might help only during climbing. The speed specificity applies only to the weight-lifting (concentric) phase of the exercise. The weight-lowering (eccentric) phase should always be slow and in control. (These types of movements are described in more detail in the sidebar entitled "Types of movements.") It is also important to be aware that if the load is too light, you will spend a large part of the lifting phase trying to slow down the weight, resulting in a decreased lifting range and decreased muscle use.

In all types of movements, be aware that improper form, overly aggressive exercise, or inadequate conditioning can result in muscle soreness that requires some type of therapeutic action. The sidebar "Delayed-onset muscle soreness" discusses various treatment options for sore muscles.

LIFTING PHASES

Developing the strength you require entails two different stages of lifting: *hypertrophy* and *strength*.

Over the short term, hypertrophy lifting may increase strength without causing large increases in muscle size or bulk.

Hypertrophy

Hypertrophy, or muscle growth, has been thought to occur with 8–12 repetitions per set. Over the short term, this sort of lifting may increase strength without causing large increases in muscle size or bulk.[15] The gains in strength may be due to increased connections between the muscle fibers and the nerves that stimulate them.[16] The benefits from this type of lifting are increased strength from increased muscle-fiber size and nerve-muscle connections.

The lifting in this phase is performed with 3 sets of 8–12 repetitions.[17] If you can do more than 12 reps of a particular weight or you are unable to complete 8 reps, adjust resistance until you fall into the 8–12 range. Increase the resistance whenever you are able, as long as every weight change is an increase.

TABLE 7.2 Hypertrophy-phase log

SET	EXERCISES	Session 1	2	3	4	5	6
	Reps			12 PER SESSION			
	Sets			3 PER SESSION			
1	Leg press						
	Crunches						
2	Leg press						
	Crunches						
3	Leg press						
	Crunches						
1	Squats						
	Leg raise						
2	Squats						
	Leg raise						
3	Squats						
	Leg raise						
1	Arm pushing						
	Arm pulling						
2	Arm pushing						
	Arm pulling						
3	Arm pushing						
	Arm pulling						
1	Back extension						
2	Back extension						
3	Back extension						

ADJUSTING THE WEIGHT:

If you can do 1-2 reps more > Add 5 lbs   If you fall short by 1-2 reps > Subtract 5 lbs
              3-4 reps more > Add 10 lbs   3-4 reps > Subtract 10 lbs
              5-6 reps more > Add 15 lbs   5-6 reps > Subtract 15 lbs

Session	7	8	9	10	11	12
Reps			12 PER SESSION			
Sets			3 PER SESSION			

SET	EXERCISES						
1	Leg press						
	Crunches						
2	Leg press						
	Crunches						
3	Leg press						
	Crunches						
1	Squats						
	Leg raise						
2	Squats						
	Leg raise						
3	Squats						
	Leg raise						
1	Arm pushing						
	Arm pulling						
2	Arm pushing						
	Arm pulling						
3	Arm pushing						
	Arm pulling						
1	Back extension						
2	Back extension						
3	Back extension						

The hypertrophy period (Table 7.2 shows a typical log) can last up to 6 weeks without significant weight gain, but you should see an increase in muscle force after 3–4 weeks.

Strength

Building strength upon a solid foundation of muscle growth and nerve-muscle connections requires decreasing the number of reps to the range of 2–6 and increasing the weight. Unlike the previous phase, where the weight was increased throughout the entire period, strength lifting is best accomplished through a weekly cycling of weight known as *daily undulating periodization* (DUP).[18] The DUP cycle requires using 3 days a week for lifting, each day separated by a rest day or a light but effective workout (see Chapter 9 for lipolysis or mitochondria biogenesis workout). On the first lifting day, perform 3 sets of 8 repetitions at the 8 rep maximum (8RM). The next lifting day, do 3 sets at 6RM. On the third lifting day, increase the weight to 3 sets at 4RM. By the time you start the cycle again the following week, the 8RM you used previously will feel too light, and you should be able to increase the resistance.

A sample week of daily undulating periodization might look like this:

Day	Bike	Sets	Reps	Weight
1		3	8	8RM
2	Lip			
3		3	6	6RM
4	Mito			
5		3	4	4RM
6	Rest/recover			
7	Rest/recover			

If you have lifted weights before, I think you will be surprised at how quickly you can make strength gains using DUP. Table 7.3 shows a typical log for the strength phase.

THE EXERCISES

Training for cycling uses strength from four distinct zones of motion: arm pushing, arm pulling, core stabilization, and leg extension. Targeting these zones with your resistance-training exercises will maximize your time in the gym.

I have selected exercises that are based primarily on multijoint movements. Unless you are trying to increase the size and strength of a particular muscle, multijoint exercises are preferred for their ability to work the whole arm or leg at once, which more closely resembles what happens when pedaling. The lifting (concentric) motion should be quick, with a slow lowering (eccentric) motion.

If you choose to add single-joint exercises, do them after the multijoint exercises. Single-joint exercises use less weight and will not tire you as much as the multijoint exercises.

When designing a weight program, pick two lower-body multijoint exercises, an upper-body pulling exercise, an upper-body pushing exercise, and abdominal and back exercises.

To maximize your time in the gym, you can do lower-body sets alternated with upper-body sets, then alternate abdominal and back exercises.

For example, alternate a set of leg presses and a set of horizontal pull-ups until you have completed all the sets, then move on to alternate sets of squats and stability-ball push-ups until you have completed all the sets for each of those exercises. Last, alternate a set of abdominal exercises with back exercises until completed.

TABLE 7.3 Strength-phase log

Session	1	2	3	4	5	6
Reps	N8	6	4	8	6	4
Sets	3 PER SESSION					

SET	EXERCISES						
1							
2	Leg press						
3							
1							
2	Squats						
3							
1							
2	Arm pushing						
3							
1							
2	Arm pulling						
3							

Maximum	Reps	12 PER SESSION					
	Sets	3 PER SESSION					
1							
2	Back extension						
3							
1							
2	Crunches						
3							
1							
2	Leg raise						
3							

ADJUSTING THE WEIGHT:

If you can do 1-2 reps more > Add 5 lbs	If you fall short by 1-2 reps > Subtract 5 lbs
3-4 reps more > Add 10 lbs	3-4 reps > Subtract 10 lbs
5-6 reps more > Add 15 lbs	5-6 reps > Subtract 15 lbs

Session	7	8	9	10	11	12
Reps	8	6	4	8	6	4
Sets			3 PER SESSION			

SET	EXERCISES						
1							
2	Leg press						
3							
1							
2	Squats						
3							
1							
2	Arm pushing						
3							
1							
2	Arm pulling						
3							

Maximum	Reps			12 PER SESSION			
	Sets			3 PER SESSION			
1							
2	Back extension						
3							
1							
2	Crunches						
3							
1							
2	Leg raise						
3							

Upper-Body Pulling

This exercise mimics the strength you need when climbing or sprinting out of the saddle. Because most cyclists have relatively weak upper bodies, exercises that use body weight are usually sufficient. Furthermore, upper-body training may need only one set to be effective.[19]

Horizontal pull-ups

Adjust the bar of a squat rack or Smith machine so that it is slightly higher than a stability ball. Hold the bar face up while resting your feet on the ball. Pull yourself toward the bar (Photos 7.1a and b).

PHOTO 7.1a   PHOTO 7.1b

PHOTO 7.2a

PHOTO 7.2b

Pull-ups

The advantage of pull-ups is that you can perform them almost anywhere; you do not need special gym equipment. With your palms facing away from you, and your body hanging straight up and down (but legs bent), pull yourself up until your chin is level with the bar (Photos 7.2a and b).

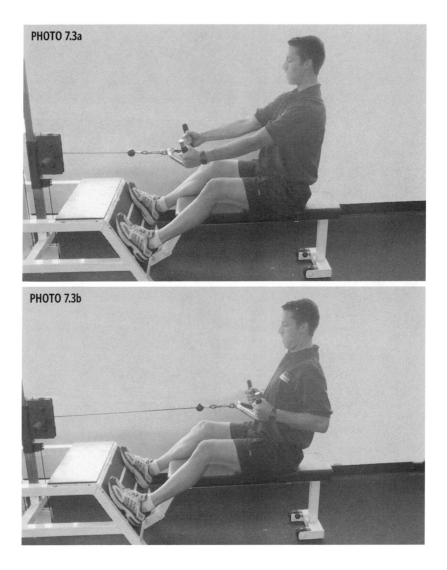

PHOTO 7.3a

PHOTO 7.3b

Seated row

Adjust the height of the pulley so that it is level with your chest. Pull the handle toward you, contracting your back (Photos 7.3a and b). Do not pull by arching your back but rather by squeezing the shoulder blades together.

Upper-Body Pushing

When the bicycle is pointing downhill, more of your weight is on your arms. This is also a time of higher speeds. Thus you need to be well supported during this time. Developing the arm-pushing muscles will allow you to descend with more control. I use a series of push-ups to help gain this strength.

Standard push-up

Place your hands on the floor shoulder-width apart. With your body rigid, move your body up and down by bending and straightening your elbows. Keep your head in line with your body and focus on a point in front of you.

PHOTO 7.4a

PHOTO 7.4b

PHOTO 7.5a

PHOTO 7.6

PHOTO 7.5b

Medicine-ball push-up

Assume the standard push-up position, except place your hands on a medicine ball. Perform a push-up (Photos 7.5a and b). For an added challenge, place one hand on the medicine ball and the other on the floor. In between push-ups, push off the ball and switch hand positions (Photo 7.6).

PHOTO 7.7a

PHOTO 7.7b

Stability-ball push-up

With your feet on a stability ball and your hands on the floor, do push-ups as previously described (Photos 7.7a and b).

Lower Body: Multiple Joint

Hack squat

Although resistance-training purists tout the virtues of free weights, I believe the well-trained cyclist can lift a lot of weight and is better suited for a machine. The hack-squat machine helps you move in a natural arc and also supports your back (Photos 7.8a and b). Raise the weight by straightening your knees. Lower the weight so that your knees bend to a 90-degree angle. Be sure not to move your knees beyond the plane of your toes.

PHOTO 7.8a

PHOTO 7.8b

Leg press

Lie on your back on the leg-press machine. Adjusting the angle of the back rest to lift your back away from the ground will use your buttock muscles more; lying flatter will engage your quadriceps more (Photos 7.9a and b). The "glutes" are the larger, stronger muscles and the ones you want to use. Lift the weight by straightening at the knees and hips; lower the weight by returning to the starting position. There is no need to bend your knees past 90 degrees.

PHOTO 7.9a

PHOTO 7.9b

Lower Body: Single Joint

Generally, single-joint exercises are not that useful for cyclists doing weight training, but two in particular can be helpful. They should be done only in the early part of the lifting program, for no more than two weeks. Frequently in cyclists, the inner part of the thigh muscles is underdeveloped, and these exercises can help work out the imbalance.

Knee extension

Seated in the machine with the pivot point even with the knee joint, straighten your leg so that it is straight out but not locked (Photos 7.10a, b, c). It is important that you work the last 30 degrees of the range of motion, as this will strengthen the weaker section of the thigh. For the lifting phase, keep your toes pointed outward. As you lower the weight, point your toes inward.

PHOTO 7.10b

PHOTO 7.10a

PHOTO 7.10c

PHOTO 7.11a

PHOTO 7.11b

PHOTO 7.12

Hamstring curls

If you are doing knee extensions to work the quadriceps at the front of the thigh, you should also strengthen the hamstrings, which are on the back of the thigh. There are several different types of hamstring-curl machines. I prefer the seated machine. For this exercise, sit in the machine with one pad above the knee and one pad behind the lower calf. Bend the knee to lift the weight (Photos 7.11a and b). For this exercise, be sure you move the leg through the full range of motion. This exercise can also be done lying face down on a different machine (Photo 7.12).

Core Strength

A tripod of muscles supports your body. These three columns of muscle are the abdominal muscles and the left and right columns of muscle in the back that run along each side of the spine. These central muscles are known as core muscles.

> **"You can't fire a cannon from a rowboat." . . . You need a stable platform to support the movement of your legs.**

A strong core will provide a solid platform from which to launch strong movements from your arms and legs. If you are not well supported, pushing on the pedals with your legs will cause your torso to move and not your pedal. As the saying goes, "You can't fire a cannon from a rowboat." In other words, you need a stable platform to support the movement of your legs.

Core strength will help you to maintain a flat, or "neutral," back that is neither curved forward nor curved backward. A neutral back will help to prevent strain in your back. Unlike the other muscles used in cycling, which alternately contract and relax, strong core muscles are continuously contracted. Training core muscles should be targeted at the endurance end of the spectrum, around 15 reps per set.

Back extensions

Using a back-extension stand, position the pad so that it is just below your pelvis. Bend forward at the waist and extend your back so that it is in line with your legs (Photos 7.13a and b). Do not extend past this point. If you feel you can do more than 15 reps, you can add resistance by holding a barbell or a weight plate against your chest.

Back extensions on stability ball

These back extensions are performed with your thighs resting on a stability ball (Photo 7.14). Your feet can be placed against a wall for extra support.

PHOTO 7.13a

PHOTO 7.13b

PHOTO 7.14

Abdominal Muscles

The rectus abdominus is a series of six muscles in the middle of your abdomen that run from the pubic bone to the rib cage. These are the muscles that contract first to stabilize your legs so that you can push against the pedals.

Upper abs: crunches

Although crunches can be done on the floor, the best way to do crunches is to isolate the abdominal muscles by bending the legs. I prefer to do this by placing a stability ball under the lower back (Photos 7.15a and b). To add resistance, you can use a cable pull at shoulder level or hold barbells on your chest. Exhale as you contract your abdominal muscles and lift your torso forward.

PHOTO 7.15a

PHOTO 7.15b

Lower abs: leg raises

Lie on the floor with your hands under your lower back for support. While keeping your legs straight, raise them off the floor until they are perpendicular to your torso (Photos 7.16a and b). To add resistance, grab a barbell or medicine ball between your feet (Photo 7.17).

PHOTO 7.16a

PHOTO 7.16b

PHOTO 7.17

Oblique abdominal muscles

These muscles run diagonally across the sides of the abdomen. They are not cycling-specific but are used for support during twisting movements. Because they are used to support your activity during crunches and leg raises, I haven't included any extra oblique exercises here. If you are interested, you should contact a personal trainer.

SUMMARY ▪ Resistance training can increase power, endurance, and recovery.

▪ Approach weight training with specific goals in order to increase strength without developing unnecessary muscle bulk.

▪ Make the most of your lifting time by using multijoint exercises.

▪ Core strengthening helps to give a more powerful pedal stroke.

NOTES

1. J.P. Ahtiainen, A. Pakarinen, M. Alen, W.J. Kraemer, K. Hakkinen. 2003. Muscle hypertrophy, hormonal adaptations and strength development during strength training in strength-trained and untrained men. *European Journal of Applied Physiology* 89, 6 (August):555-63.

2. M. Ross. 2003. *Maximum Performance: Sports Medicine for Endurance Athletes.* VeloPress: Boulder, CO.

3. H. Tanaka and T. Swensen. 1998. Impact of resistance training on endurance performance: A new form of cross-training. *Sports Medicine* 25, 3 (March):191-200.

4. G.E. Campos, T.J. Luecke, H.K. Wendeln, K. Toma, F.C. Hagerman, T.F. Murray, K.E. Ragg, N.A. Ratamess, W.J. Kraemer, and R.S. Staron. 2002. Muscular adaptations in response to three different resistance-training regimens: Specificity of repetition maximum training zones. *European Journal of Applied Physiology* 88, 1–2 (November):50–60.

J. Hoff, A. Gran, and J. Helgerud. 2002. Maximal strength training improves aerobic endurance performance. *Scandinavian Journal of Medicine and Science in Sports* 12, 5 (October):288–95.

5. R.H. Fitts and J.J. Widrick. 1996. Muscle mechanics: Adaptations with exercise-training. *Exercise and Sport Science Review* 24 (1996):427–73.

6. Hoff et al. 2002.

7. G.J. Bell, D. Syrotuik, T.P. Martin, R. Burnham, and H.A. Quinney. 2000. Effect of concurrent strength and endurance training on skeletal muscle properties and hormone concentrations in humans. *European Journal of Applied Physiology* 81, 5 (March):418–27.

8. J.P. Folland, C.S. Irish, J.C. Roberts, J.E. Tarr, and D.A. Jones. 2002. Fatigue is not a necessary stimulus for strength gains during resistance training. *British Journal of Sports Medicine* 36, 5 (October):370–3.

9. Campos et al. 2002.

10. R.W. Braith, J.E. Graves, M.L. Pollock, S.L. Leggett, D.M. Carpenter, and A.B. Colvin. 1989. Comparison of 2 vs 3 days/week of variable resistance training during 10- and 18-week programs. *International Journal of Sports Medicine* 10, 6 (December):450–4.

11. W.J. Kraemer, N.D. Duncan, and J.S. Volek. 1998. Resistance training and elite athletes: Adaptations and program considerations. *Journal of Orthopedic Sports and Physical Therapy* 28, 2 (August):110–9.

12. G.J. Wilson, A.J. Murphy, and A. Walshe. 1996. The specificity of strength training: The effect of posture. *European Journal of Applied Physiology and Occupational Physiology* 73(3–4):346–52.

13. J.L. Ewing Jr., D.R. Wolfe, M.A. Rogers, M.L. Amundson, and G.A. Stull. 1990. Effects of velocity of isokinetic training on strength, power, and quadriceps muscle fibre characteristics. *European Journal of Applied Physiology and Occupational Physiology* 61 (1–2):159–62.

K. Jones, P. Bishop, G. Hunter, and G. Fleisig. 2001. The effects of varying resistance-training loads on intermediate- and high-velocity-specific adaptations. *Journal of Strength and Conditioning Research* 15, 3 (August):349–56.

D. Paddon-Jones, M. Leveritt, A. Lonergan, and P. Abernethy. 2001. Adaptation to chronic eccentric exercise in humans: The influence of contraction velocity. *European Journal of Applied Physiology* 85, 5 (September):466–71.

14. H. Kanehisa and M. Miyashita. 1983. Specificity of velocity in strength training. *European Journal of Applied Physiology and Occupational Physiology* 52(1):104–6.

15. P. Brandenburg and D. Docherty. 2002. The effects of accentuated eccentric loading on strength, muscle hypertrophy, and neural adaptations in trained individuals. *Journal of Strength and Conditioning Research* 16, 1 (February):25–32.

16. E.G. Colliander and P.A. Tesch. 1990. Effects of eccentric and concentric muscle actions in resistance training. *Acta Physiologica Scandinavia* 140, 1 (September):31–9.

K. Hakkinen, M. Kallinen, P.V. Komi, and H. Kauhanen. 1991. Neuromuscular adaptations during short-term "normal" and reduced training periods in strength athletes. *Electromyogr Clin Neurophysiol* 31, 1 (January–February):35–42.

17. G. Paulsen, D. Myklestad, and T. Raastad. 2003. The influence of volume of exercise on early adaptations to strength training. *Journal of Strength and Conditioning Research* 17, 1 (February):115–20.

18. M.R. Rhea, S.D. Ball, W.T. Phillips, and L.N. Burkett. 2002. A comparison of linear and daily undulating periodized programs with equated volume and intensity for strength. *Journal of Strength and Conditioning Research* 16, 2 (May):250–5.

19. Paulsen et al. 2003.

FLEXIBILITY 8

When I first started cycling, my coach told me that cyclists did not need flexibility. "I haven't touched my toes in years," he joked. This attitude was prevalent throughout the national team and professional ranks, but perspectives have changed quite a bit since then. A focus on flexibility has become more accepted as activities such as yoga and tai chi chuan have gained popularity and yielded improved flexibility in those who practice them.[1]

Flexibility is not just a passing trend, however. Flexibility is needed to achieve proper position on the bicycle and is important in decreasing many of the common overuse injuries of the knee, back, and ankle that are encountered during cycling. The flexible athlete also will have decreased muscle soreness after workouts.[2]

WHAT IS FLEXIBILITY?

Flexibility, although frequently overlooked, is one of the main components of physical fitness, along with strength, muscular endurance, cardiovascular endurance, and body composition. Good flexibility is what determines the range of motion in a joint. It enables you to produce greater force by having the muscle stretched before it contracts.

Like strength and power, the flexibility needed for cycling has a time component. Static flexibility, such as touching your toes, lacks a time component. In contrast, dynamic flexibility, which is what you need to develop for cycling, is a matter of how quickly you need a range of motion. Given enough time, even cyclists with very tight hamstrings can touch their toes. However, if the action needs to be performed quickly by someone with decreased flexibility, it could cause pain and injury. The gradual stretching of muscles is important because of their *viscoelasticity.*

There are four ways to stretch: passive, passive with an assist, dynamic, and proprioceptive neuromuscular facilitation. *Passive* stretching is simply assuming a position and holding it to stretch a muscle. *Passive* stretching *with an assist* is the same except a partner helps you to achieve a position that is more of a stretch than you could manage alone. With this type of stretching, it is important to go slowly and communicate well to prevent an injury. *Dynamic,* or ballistic, stretching uses bouncing movements to stretch farther and farther. Dynamic stretching is associated with a high rate of injury and decreased strength, and I therefore do not recommend it.[3] Finally, *proprioceptive neuromuscular facilitation* (PNF) is a method of achieving increased flexibility by alternating muscle stretching and muscle contraction.

Viscoelasticity

Muscles are neither elastic (snaps back when tension is released) nor plastic (remains in whatever position they are placed) but rather are viscoelastic. Viscoelasticity is best explained by imagining the stress-relieving toys that can be pounded and tugged upon but slowly regain their original shape. Like those toys, the muscles can be stretched slowly into new positions, but unless frequently stretched, they will return to their original length.

HOW TO STRETCH

Passive (static) stretching is the simplest method to increase flexibility, since it can be done alone. Stretching should be done after the muscles have been warmed up from exercise, not before. To perform a static stretch, assume the position and increase the stretch until you feel slight tightness of the muscle in which you are trying to increase flexibility. It is important to stop before you feel any pain. As you hold the stretch, the muscle will start to relax. When this occurs, the stretch feeling will disperse. If the feeling of stretch increases, you have gone too far and need to back off. A little less is probably better than too much.

At the point of relaxation, increase the stretch. Hold each stretch for 30 seconds.[4] Holding a stretch beyond 30 seconds is not effective. If you want to increase flexibility further, repeat the stretching at different times during the day or even in the same workout session, as it is the total daily stretch time that matters.[5] The key to increased flexibility is consistency. If you discontinue and restart your stretching routine, you are likely to lose any benefits of stretching.[6]

The body (including the jaw) should be relaxed; breathing should be slow and deep.

PNF is most effective after exercise.[7] To perform PNF, assume a stretching position and increase the stretch, stopping before the point of pain. Next, contract the muscle that you are stretching for 10 seconds,[8] and then relax the muscle and increase the stretch. You should be able to stretch to a point greater than where you were before the contraction. It is easier to perform PNF stretching with a partner who can help with passive stretching and resisting your muscle contractions. Photos 8.7a and b illustrate PNF for a hamstring stretch.

Lower-Leg Stretches

Calf

Face a wall at arm's length and place one foot forward. To stretch muscles of the calf in back, lean into the wall (Photo 8.1). Switch foot position to stretch the other side.

Deep calf

Start with the same position as the calf stretch and after stretching the calf, bend both knees to increase the stretch (Photo 8.2). Switch foot position to stretch the other side.

Standing calf stretch

Bend the knees and lean forward at the ankles. You will feel tension in the calf and you will feel the quadriceps contract (Photo 8.3). This action not only will stretch the Achilles tendon but also will relax the hamstrings, getting them ready to be stretched.

PHOTO 8.1

PHOTO 8.2

Upper-Leg Stretches

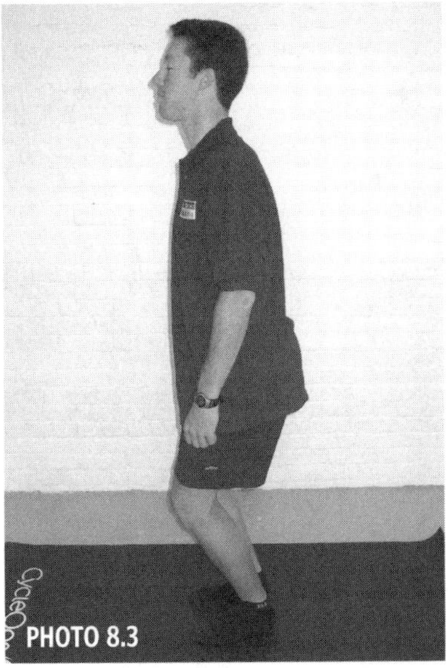

The hamstrings are several muscles in the back of the thigh and are usually tight in cyclists. Increased hamstring flexibility will allow you to get into a lower, more aerodynamic position as well as decrease some of the overuse injuries in the knee. To stretch these muscles effectively, I use several different stretches.

Isolated-hamstring stretch

While seated on the floor, place the right leg straight out with the knee slightly bent and put the sole of the left foot against the inside of the right thigh. Bend forward at the waist (Photo 8.4a). If you are unable to touch your toes, use a towel to help you stretch (Photos 8.4b). Keep the quadriceps relaxed. Switch legs and stretch the other side.

PHOTO 8.3

PHOTO 8.4a

PHOTO 8.4b

Straight-leg raise

Lying on your back with the left leg straight out, raise the right leg by bending at the hip until you feel tightness in the back of the thigh (Photo 8.5). If this position does not produce a stretch, pull the leg toward you. Keep the ankle at 90 degrees for maximum stretch. Switch legs to stretch the other side.

PHOTO 8.5

Figure 4 stretch

Lie on your back and cross your legs so that one ankle is on top of the other knee. Wrap your hands under the back leg and pull toward you (Photo 8.6). You will feel the stretch in the buttock of the leg being pulled and in the hamstring of the crossed leg. Switch legs to stretch the other side.

PHOTO 8.6

PNF hamstring stretch

PNF stretching has been shown to increase hamstring flexibility. While lying on your back with the right leg bent 90 degrees at the hip, pull the leg toward you until you feel a stretch in the hamstring (Photo 8.7a). Contract the hamstring by pushing the leg into a stationary object, either a chair, a partner, or a towel you are holding (Photos 8.7b). Hold this contraction for 10 seconds, release, and repeat the stretch, pulling the leg to a new limit of tension. Switch legs to stretch the other side.

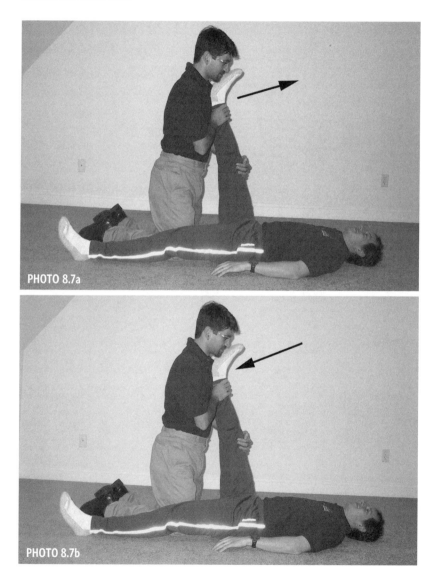

PHOTO 8.7a

PHOTO 8.7b

Quadriceps

Stand on the right leg, bend the left knee, and grab the top of the foot with the right hand. If you need extra balance, brace yourself against a wall with your free hand. Pull the foot up and back to achieve the desired stretch (Photo 8.8). Switch legs to stretch the other side.

Iliotibial-band stretch

Stand with your side to the wall and lean against the wall with your arm for support. Cross the outside leg over the inside leg; be sure to keep the foot of the outside leg flat on the floor. Move the hips toward the wall and apply pressure from the outside hand to the hips (Photo 8.9). This will stretch the ITB of the inside leg. Switch legs to stretch the other side.

PHOTO 8.8   PHOTO 8.9

External-rotator stretch

Lie on your back and bend one knee up to your chest. Use the opposite hand to pull the knee across to the opposite side of the chest (Photo 8.10). Switch legs to stretch the other side.

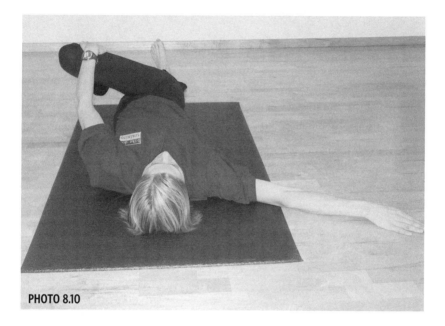

PHOTO 8.10

SUMMARY ■ Maintain flexibility with a daily stretching routine and you will notice that you have increased power on the bike, decreased injury frequency, and improved position.

■ Stretching is most effective after a workout when the muscles are warm and most flexible.

■ Stretching should not be part of a warm-up.

■ Passive stretching is the easiest method of stretching.

■ Hold each stretch for 30 seconds at a time for maximum benefit.

NOTES

1. Y. Hong, J.X. Li, and P.D. Robinson. 2000. Balance control, flexibility, and cardiorespiratory fitness among older Tai Chi practitioners. *British Journal of Sports Medicine* 34, 1 (February):29–34.

J.A. Raub. 2002. Psychophysiologic effects of Hatha Yoga on musculoskeletal and cardiopulmonary function: A literature review. *Journal of Alternative and Complementary Medicine* 8, 6 (December):797–812.

2. S. Bryant. 1984. Flexibility and stretching. *The Physician and Sports Medicine* 12 (2):171.

3. A.G. Nelson and J. Kokkonen. 2001. Acute ballistic muscle stretching inhibits maximal strength performance. *Research Quarterly for Exercise and Sport* 72, 4 (December):415–9.

4. W.D. Bandy and J.M. Irion. 1994. The effect of time on static stretch on the flexibility of the hamstring muscles. *Physical Therapy* 74, 9 (September):845–50.

W.D. Bandy, J.M. Irion, and M. Briggler. 1997. The effect of time and frequency of static stretching on flexibility of the hamstring muscles. *Physical Therapy* 77, 10 (September):1090–6.

5. D. Cipriani, B. Abel, and D. Pirrwitz. 2003. A comparison of two stretching protocols on hip range of motion: Implications for total daily stretch duration. *Journal of Strength and Conditioning Research* 17, 2 (May):274–8.

6. R.W. Willy, B.A. Kyle, S.A. Moore, and G.S. Chleboun. 2001. Effect of cessation and resumption of static hamstring muscle stretching on joint range of motion. *The Journal of Orthopedic and Sports Physical Therapy* 31, 3 (March):138–44.

7. D.C. Funk, A.M. Swank, B.M. Mikla, T.A. Fagan, and B.K. Farr. 2003. Impact of prior exercise on hamstring flexibility: A comparison of proprioceptive neuromuscular facilitation and static stretching. *Journal of Strength and Conditioning Research* 17, 3 (August):489–92.

8. A.V. Rowlands, V.F. Marginson, and J. Lee. 2003. Chronic flexibility gains: Effect of isometric contraction duration during proprioceptive neuromuscular facilitation stretching techniques. *Research Quarterly for Exercise and Sport* 74, 1 (March):47–51.

WORKOUTS 9

LOW-INTENSITY WORKOUTS

Repair (R)

Goal: To improve muscle recovery by using the natural pumping motion of the legs to clear metabolic waste products such as lactic acid.

Gear: Easy.

Cadence: Above preferred.

How to: Select a 45-minute flat course. The ride should be done seated.

Intensity: Heart rate zones 1–2.

Volume: 45 minutes.

Nutrition: Before › 500ml of 6% carbohydrate solution.

During › 500–1200ml of 6% carbohydrate solution.

After › A ratio of 3:1, carbohydrate-protein smoothie immediately and at 1 hour after the ride.

Low-Intensity Training (Lit)

Goal: To prime the secretion of recovery hormones, increase mitochondria, and promote capillary growth.

Gear: As needed.

Cadence: Preferred.

How to: Ride at a low to moderate intensity.

Intensity: Heart rate zones 2–3.

Power: Up to 70% of critical power.

Volume: Beginners › 2 hours.

Previously trained › up to 4 hours.

Nutrition: Before › Preride meal, 500ml carbohydrate-electrolyte beverage.

During › 600–1200ml carbohydrate-electrolyte beverage.

After › A 3:1 ratio, carbohydrate-protein meal immediately and 1 hour after ride.

RACE WARM-UP

Goal: To increase the lactic acid and temperature of the muscles to improve function and oxygen delivery.

Gear: As needed.

Cadence: Preferred or above preferred.

How to: Start riding in heart rate zone 2 and spin until the movement becomes easier. When this happens, increase to zone 3 for 5 minutes and then to zone 4 for 5 minutes. Arrive at the start line as soon as possible after finishing the warm-up. Warm-up benefits dissipate quickly, especially if it is cold.

Intensity: Heart rate zones 2–4.

Power: Not applicable.

Volume: 15–20 minutes.

Nutrition: Before › Prerace meal.

During › 500ml of carbohydrate-electrolyte beverage.

After › Race nutrition: 500–1200ml of carbohydrate-electrolyte beverage each hour.

WARM-UP

Goal: To increase the lactic acid and temperature of the muscles to improve function and oxygen delivery.

Gear: As needed.

Cadence: Preferred or above preferred.

How to: Start riding in heart rate zone 2 and spin until the movement becomes easier. When this happens, increase to zone 3 for 5 minutes and then to zone 4 for 5 minutes.

Intensity: Heart rate zones 2–4.

Power: Not applicable.

Volume: 15–20 minutes.

Nutrition: Before › Preride meal.

During › 500ml of carbohydrate-electrolyte beverage.

After › Follow specific nutritional guidelines for each workout.

Warm-up Drills

Progressive muscular relaxation

Grip the handlebars as tightly as possible, feeling the tension. Relax completely, feeling the tension leave the hands, and silently repeat "relax" or "smooth" or "liquid speed" (cues) as you relax. Next, tense the forearms and upper arms as tightly as you can, hold for 3 seconds, and relax completely, repeating the cue word or phrase that you associate with relaxation. Contract the shoulders, bringing them up to your ears, hold 3 seconds, and relax while repeating the cue word. Curl the shoulders inward, tense, hold, and relax and repeat the cue word. Continue with the warm-up and repeat the cue word and relax every minute.

Spin-ups

After reaching zone 4 in the warm-up, shift into an easy gear and increase cadence to maximum. Place keys or loose change in your back pocket and avoid bouncing by preventing the keys from jingling.

COOL-DOWN

Goal: To use the natural pumping action of the legs to help clear lactic acid after a workout.[1]

Gear: Easy.

Cadence: Above preferred.

How to: After completion of a workout.

Intensity: Heart rate zone 1.

Power: 50% critical power.

Volume: 20 minutes.

Nutrition: Before › Specific nutrition for the workout you were doing.

During › 200–400 of a carbohydrate-electrolyte solution.

After › A 3:1 ratio, carbohydrate and protein immediately after and then again at one hour after.

Cool-down Drills

Shadow biking

While riding in an easy gear, position yourself so that the sun is behind you. Stand on the pedals and rock the bike from side to side as you would do while climbing or sprinting. Study your shadow. The shadow of your torso should not move from side to side as the bicycle moves beneath you. It is best to perform this drill after a workout when you would be tired. Shadow biking will train you to stabilize your core and use it as a platform to increase power to the pedals.

Corners

After a workout, find some slight downhill corners and practice taking different lines through them. Find a lean angle (that is, your bicycle forms a narrow angle with the ground) that you are comfortable with and try to increase speed through the corners. As you lean the bike, keep the torso upright with the outside pedal down.

Obstacles

Set up small obstacles and practice "bunny hopping" over them. If you can't get the whole bike over them, try lifting the front wheel by pulling up on the handlebars and leaning back. Then quickly lift the back wheel by pushing down on the handlebars and shifting your weight forward.

Descending

Find a descent and ride down it. Keep the upper body relaxed and use your cue word to help with relaxation.

LIPOLYSIS WORKOUTS

Lipolysis 1 (Lip1)

Goal: To develop increased use of fat as an energy source during easy and moderate riding. This is a good workout to use in between resistance training days.

Gear: As needed.

Cadence: Freely chosen cadence.

How to: Do this ride shortly after waking up and on an empty stomach. Start riding with a heart rate in zone 2 and increase rapidly to zone 3.

Set the timer for 1 hour. Stop at 1 hour. If you are not near home, have carbohydrate and protein at 1 hour. If you smell ammonia on your breath at any time, stop and eat immediately. If you notice a significant decrease in power output, stop and eat immediately.

Intensity: Heart rate zone 3.

Volume: 1 hour maximum.

Nutrition: Before ⟩ 500ml water. Branched-chain amino acid supplement is optional but can help prevent muscle breakdown. Caffeinated beverage without sugar is optional.

During ⟩ 500–1200ml water and branched-chain amino acid supplement.

After ⟩ A 3:1 ratio, carbohydrate-protein smoothie immediately and at 1 hour after the ride.

Lipolysis 2 (Lip2)

Goal: To develop increased use of fat as an energy source in type IIa muscle fibers.

Gear: As needed.

Cadence: Preferred.

How to: Do this ride shortly after waking up and on an empty stomach. Keep your power just below 80% of critical power. Set the timer for 1 hour. Stop at 1 hour. If you are not near home, have carbohydrate and protein at 1 hour. If you smell ammonia on your breath at any time, stop and eat immediately. If you notice a significant decrease in power output, stop and eat immediately.

Power: 75–80% critical power.

Intensity: Just below Heart rate zone 80-85.

Volume: 1 hour maximum.

Nutrition: Before › 500ml water. Caffeinated beverage without sugar
is optional.

During › 500–1200ml water.

After › 3:1 ratio, carbohydrate-protein smoothie immediately and
at 1 hour after the ride.

MITOCHONDRIAL BIOGENESIS WORKOUTS

Mitochondrial Biogenesis 1 (Mito1)

Goal: To increase the number of mitochondria, the powerhouse and energy
factory of the muscle cell.

Gear: As needed.

Cadence: Preferred.

Intensity: Heart-rate zones 3–4.

Volume: one hour.

How to: First thing after waking in the morning, ride for one hour. If you
smell ammonia on your breath at any time, stop and eat immediately. If
you notice a significant decrease in power output, stop and eat immediately.

Nutrition: Before › 500ml water. Branched-chain amino acid supplement
is optional but can help prevent muscle breakdown. Caffeinated
beverage without sugar is optional.

During › 500–1200ml water.

After › A 3:1 ratio, carbohydrate-protein smoothie immediately and
at one hour after the ride.

Mitochondrial Biogenesis 2 (Mito2)

Goal: To increase the number of mitochondria, the powerhouse of the
muscle cell.

Gear: As needed.

Cadence: Lower than preferred.

Intensity: At or slightly above the lactate threshold power or heart rate.

Power: 91% of critical power.

Volume: 1 hour.

How to: Ride for 1 hour. If you smell ammonia on your breath at any time, stop and eat immediately. If you notice a significant decrease in power output, stop and eat immediately.

Nutrition: Before › 500ml water. Branched-chain amino acid supplement is optional but can help prevent muscle breakdown. Caffeinated beverage without sugar is optional.

During › 500–1200ml water.

After › A 3:1 ratio, carbohydrate-protein smoothie immediately and at 1 hour after the ride.

Mitochondrial Biogenesis 3 (Mito3)

Goal: To increase the number of mitochondria, the powerhouse of the muscle cell.

Gear: As needed.

Cadence: Preferred.

Intensity: Phase I › Heart rate zones 2–3.

Phase II › Heart rate zones 4–5.

Volume: 2–2.5 hours.

How to: Phase I › Spend the first 1.5 hours of the ride in heart rate zones 2–3.

Phase II › After 1.5 hours, start to increase the intensity to above the lactate threshold heart rate. Perform length intervals of 1 minute. Intervals will be 1 minute, 2 minutes, 3 minutes, 2 minutes, 1 minutes. If you are still producing power, repeat the sequence until your power declines, or you are unable to increase your heart rate.

Nutrition: Before › Preride meal, 500ml carbohydrate-electrolyte beverage.

During › 600–1200ml carbohydrate-electrolyte beverage.

After › A 3:1 ratio, carbohydrate-protein meal immediately and 1 hour after ride.

Mitochondrial Biogenesis 4 (Mito4)

Goal: To increase the number of mitochondria, the powerhouse of the muscle cell, through glycogen depletion.[2]

Gear: As needed.

Cadence: Below preferred.[3]

Intensity: Heart-rate zone 4.

Volume: Warm-up plus 1 hour, 15 minutes.

How to: After warming up, ride for 1 hour at your lactate threshold heart rate. This can be accomplished by doing 4 sets of 15 minutes of work with a 5-minute break between each interval.

Nutrition: Before › 500ml water. Branched-chain amino acid supplement is optional but can help prevent muscle breakdown. Caffeinated beverage without sugar is optional.

During › 500–1200ml water per hour and branched-chain amino acid supplement.

After › 3:1 ratio, carbohydrate-protein smoothie immediately and at 1 hour after the ride.

HIGH-INTENSITY TRAINING (HIT)

To be able to ride over different terrain, you should perform HIT workouts equally on different grade hills, on rolling terrain, and on flats. If you are only doing these workouts on the same road, you will only be prepared for that road, and not for various race courses.

HIT1

Goal: To increase power through increased muscle-fiber recruitment.

Gear: As needed.

Cadence: Preferred or above.

How to: After a warm-up, perform 8 intervals at 50, 60, or 70% of Tmax. Recover half as long as the work interval.

Intensity: Heart rate not applicable.

Power: Critical power.

Volume: 8 intervals per set with 5 minutes of complete recovery between sets. You may do up to 3 sets. Stop when unable to reach critical power.

Nutrition: Before › Preride meal, 500ml carbohydrate-electrolyte beverage.

During › 600–1200ml carbohydrate-electrolyte beverage.

After › A 3:1 ratio, carbohydrate-protein meal immediately and 1 hour after.

HIT2

Goal: To increase power and 40km time-trial power through increased muscle-fiber recruitment.

Gear: As needed.

Cadence: Preferred or above.

How to: After a warm-up, perform 8 intervals at 50, 60, or 70% of Tmax. Recover to 65% of maximum heart rate.

Intensity: Heart rate not applicable.

Power: Critical power.

Volume: 8 intervals per set. You may do up to 3 sets. Stop when unable to reach critical power.

Nutrition: Before › Preride meal, 500ml carbohydrate-electrolyte beverage.

During › 600–1200ml carbohydrate-electrolyte beverage.

After › A 3:1 ratio, carbohydrate-protein meal immediately and 1 hour after.

HIT3

Goal: To increase cycling performance through maximal muscle-fiber recruitment.

Gear: As needed.

Cadence: Preferred or above.

How to: After a warm-up, perform 12 intervals, each 30 seconds long, at 175% of critical power. Recover for 4.5 minutes between each effort.

Intensity: Heart rate not applicable.

Power: 175% critical power.

Volume: 12 intervals.

Nutrition: Before › Preride meal, 500ml carbohydrate-electrolyte beverage.

During › 600–1200ml carbohydrate-electrolyte beverage.

After › A 3:1 ratio, carbohydrate-protein meal immediately and 1 hour after.

HIT4

Goal: To increase work and force production through increased muscle-fiber recruitment.

Gear: As needed.

Cadence: Preferred or above.

How to: After a warm-up, perform 20 intervals, each 60 seconds long, with 120 seconds recovery.

Intensity: Heart rate not applicable.

Power: Critical power.

Volume: 20 intervals per set. Stop after 20 intervals or if unable to reach critical power.

Nutrition: Before › Preride meal, 500ml carbohydrate-electrolyte beverage.

During › 600–1200ml carbohydrate-electrolyte beverage.

After › A 3:1 ratio, carbohydrate-protein meal immediately and 1 hour after.

HIT5

Goal: To increase time at maximum aerobic capacity and increase use of fat while sparing glycogen.

Gear: As needed.

Cadence: Preferred or above.

How to: After a warm-up, perform up to 1 hour of microintervals of 15 seconds work and 15 seconds rest.

Intensity: Heart rate not applicable.

Power: Critical power.

Volume: Up to 120 microintervals. Stop when unable to reach critical power.

Nutrition: Before › Preride meal, 500ml carbohydrate-electrolyte beverage.

During › 600–1200ml carbohydrate-electrolyte beverage.

After › A 3:1 ratio, carbohydrate-protein meal immediately and 1 hour after.

HIT6

Goal: To increase power through increased muscle-fiber recruitment.

Gear: As needed.

Cadence: Preferred or above.

How to: After a warm-up, perform 20 intervals of 30 seconds with a 30-second recovery between each interval.

Intensity: Heart rate not applicable.

Power: Critical power.

Volume: 20 intervals. Stop when unable to reach critical power.

Nutrition: Before › Preride meal, 500ml carbohydrate-electrolyte beverage.

During › 600–1200ml carbohydrate-electrolyte beverage.

After › A 3:1 ratio, carbohydrate-protein meal immediately and 1 hour after.

SUSTAINED POWER AND MUSCULAR ENDURANCE
SPAM1

Goal: To increase energy-producing capacity of type II muscle fibers.

Gear: As needed.

Cadence: Preferred or above.

How to: After a warm-up, perform 4-minute intervals with 2-minute recovery.

Intensity: Heart-rate zones 4–5 or heart rate at 80–85% of critical power.

Power: 80–85% critical power.

Volume: 6–8 intervals per set. If you are able to maintain 80–85% critical power, you may do 2 sets. Stop when you no longer can sustain power.

Nutrition: Before › Preride meal, 500ml carbohydrate-electrolyte beverage.

During › 600–1200ml carbohydrate-electrolyte beverage.

After › A 3:1 ratio, carbohydrate-protein meal immediately and 1 hour after.

SPAM2

Goal: To increase oxidative capacity of type II muscle fibers and lactic-acid buffering capacity.

Gear: As needed.

Cadence: Preferred or above.

How to: After a warm-up, perform 4-minute intervals with 1-minute recovery.

Intensity: Heart rate zones 4–5 or heart rate at 80–85% of critical power.

Power: 80–85% critical power.

Volume: 6–8 intervals per set. If you are able to maintain 80–85% critical power, you may do 2 sets. Stop when you no longer can sustain power.

Nutrition: Before › Preride meal, 500ml carbohydrate-electrolyte beverage.

During › 600–1200ml carbohydrate-electrolyte beverage.

After › A 3:1 ratio, carbohydrate-protein meal immediately and 1 hour after.

SPAM3

Goal: To increase oxidative capacity of type II muscle fibers, lactic-acid buffering capacity, and peak power and to improve 40km time-trial work.

Gear: As needed.

Cadence: Preferred or above.

How to: After a warm-up, perform 5-minute intervals with 1-minute recovery.

Intensity: Heart-rate zones 4–5 or heart rate at 80–85% of critical power.

Power: 80–85% critical power.

Volume: 6–8 intervals per set. If you are able to maintain 80–85% critical power, you may do 2 sets. Stop when you no longer can sustain power.

Nutrition: Before › Preride meal, 500ml carbohydrate-electrolyte beverage.

During › 600–1200ml carbohydrate-electrolyte beverage.

After › At 3:1 ratio, carbohydrate-protein meal immediately and 1 hour after.

POSTACTIVATION POTENTIATION (PAP)

PAP1

Goal: To increase explosive power.

Gear: Phase I › Choose a gear that you are barely able to turn.

Phase II › Choose a gear that you can turn with a high cadence.

Cadence: Phase I › Barely moving the pedals against resistance.

Phase II › Above preferred. Sprint with a high cadence.

How to: Warm up first.

Phase I › Pick a hill that plateaus or drops slightly after the top. Start on this hill in a gear that is almost too large to turn over. As you pedal, you will have near-maximal strength contractions. After 20 seconds, crest the top of the hill.

Phase II › After cresting the top of the hill, shift into an easier gear and pedal easily for 15 seconds. After this rest period, sprint as hard as you can for 10–15 seconds. If your legs are tired after the 15-second rest, try rest periods of 30, 45, and 60 seconds.

Intensity: Heart rate not applicable.

Power: Maximum power.

Volume: 6–10 sprints. Stop when your maximum power is decreasing.

Nutrition: Before › Preride meal, 500ml carbohydrate-electrolyte beverage.

During › 600–1200ml carbohydrate-electrolyte beverage.

After › At 3:1 ratio, carbohydrate-protein meal immediately and 1 hour after ride.

PAP2

Goal: To increase explosive power on hills.

Gear: Phase I › Choose a gear that you are barely able to turn.

Phase II › Choose a gear that you can turn with a high cadence.

Cadence: Phase I › Barely moving the pedals against resistance.

Phase II › Above preferred. Climb with a high cadence.

How to: Warm up first.

Phase I › Pick a steep hill that rises gradually. Start on this hill in a gear that is almost too large to turn over. As you pedal, you will have near-maximal strength contractions and a low cadence. After 20 seconds, shift into an easier gear.

Phase II › After shifting into an easier gear, continue climbing with a high cadence for 30–60 seconds. If your legs are too tired to climb in the easier gear, try a very easy gear for 15 seconds, and continue to climb with increased power after the rest period. You can try rest periods of 30 or 45 seconds if needed. Recover after the climbing interval for 2 minutes or to heart rate zone 1.

Intensity: Heart rate not applicable.

Power: 100% Critical power.

Volume: 6–10 climbs. Stop when your maximum power is decreasing.

Nutrition: Before › Preride meal, 500ml carbohydrate-electrolyte beverage.

During › 600–1200ml carbohydrate-electrolyte beverage.

After › At 3:1 ratio, carbohydrate-protein meal immediately and one hour after ride.

EXPLOSIVE STARTS

Goal: To practice starting and increase power at the beginning of a race.

Gear: Start in something easy, then increase as needed.

Cadence: High.

How to: Warm up first. Start with one foot on the ground. If training with a partner, have your partner say "Ready, set, go." Start the interval by clipping into the pedal and accelerate quickly to critical power. After 30–60 seconds at critical power, settle into a 4-minute interval at lactate threshold heart rate. Recover to zone 1.

Intensity: Lactate threshold heart rate.

Power: critical power for 30–60 seconds, then lactate threshold heart rate.

Volume: 8 intervals per set. If you are still producing critical power, you may start a second set, but stop if you are no longer producing critical power.

Nutrition: Before › Preride meal, 500ml carbohydrate-electrolyte beverage.

During › 600–1200ml carbohydrate-electrolyte beverage.

After › At 3:1 ratio, carbohydrate-protein meal immediately and 1 hour after ride.

DIETARY MANIPULATIONS TO INCREASE ENDURANCE

Fat Adapt

Goal: To increase the use of fat through 5 days of a high-fat diet.

Associated workouts: 2 hours a day for 5 days of low-intensity training at or above 65% of maximum heart rate or 65% critical power. Lipolysis (LIP) can also be used.

Duration: 5 days.

Nutrition: Before › Fat-adapt preride meal (70% fat, 15% carbohydrate, 15% protein).

During › 600–1200ml carbohydrate-electrolyte beverage.

After › Fat-adapt smoothie and postride meals.

Mitochondrial Biogenesis

Goal: To increase the function of the mitochondria glycogen-storage enzymes by depriving the mitochondria of carbohydrate.

Associated workout: Mito (any workout) followed by 3 days off.

Duration: 5 days.

Nutrition: Before › 500ml water.

During › 600–1200ml water.

After › 66 hours of low-carbohydrate meals, followed by a high-carbohydrate dinner on day 3.

Carbo-Load (CL)

Goal: To cause maximal glycogen supercompensation. This will allow increased energy stores for intensity.

How to: After a warm-up, perform 2.5 minutes at 80–90% critical power, followed immediately by a 30-second all-out effort.[4] Cool down.

Timing: 24 hours before an important event, preferably after waking up.

Nutrition: Before › 500ml water.

During › 600–1200 ml of carbohydrate-electrolyte beverage.

After › A 3:1 ratio, carbohydrate-protein smoothie immediately

followed by 12 grams of carbohydrate per kilogram of body weight over the next 24 hours.

TAPER

Goal: To maintain intensity but decrease volume to allow for extra recovery before an important event. A good taper will increase glycogen storage, strength, and mitochondria function.[5]

Workouts: HIT or SPAM.

Volume: Decrease number of usual intervals by 50–85%.[6]

Duration: 4–8 days or one training block.[7]

Nutrition: Before › Preride meal, 500ml carbohydrate-electrolyte beverage.

During › 600–1200ml carbohydrate-electrolyte beverage.

After › A 3:1 ratio, carbohydrate-protein meal immediately and 1 hour after ride.

GROUP DRILLS

Sometimes you need to ride with a group, whether it is for the company or to prevent boredom and staleness, and it can be a nice diversion from training alone. These are some good drills to try with a group:

Breakaways

Encourage the group to practice chasing a rider who has a head start. If you are feeling fit, take extra turns at the breakaway.

Sprints

When riding with a group, have one rider call out a target to sprint for (town line, mailbox). No one can start the sprint until the caller jumps. This will develop your sprint strategy and lead-out skills.

Starts

Have everyone line up shoulder-width on a quiet street. One person calls "Ready, set, go," and everyone races for 1 minute. See who can ride the farthest.

Dropbacks

If the group is moving slower than you would like, drop back and chase them down. Depending upon the lead you give them, you can do HIT or SPAM workouts this way.

NOTES

1. J. Mondero and B. Donne. 2000. Effect of recovery interventions on lactate removal and subsequent performance. *International Journal of Sports Medicine* 21, 8 (November): 593–97.

2. N.K. Vollestad and P.C. Blom. 1985. Effect of varying exercise intensity on glycogen depletion in human muscle fibres. *Acta Physiologica Scandinavia* 125, 3 (November):395–405.

3. L.E. Ahlquist, D.R. Bassett Jr., R. Sufit, F.J. Nagle, and D.P. Thomas. 1992. The effect of pedaling frequency on glycogen depletion rates in type I and type II quadriceps muscle fibers during submaximal cycling exercise. *European Journal of Applied Physiology and Occupational Physiology* 65 (4):360–4.

4. V.A. Bussau, T.J. Fairchild, A. Rao, P. Steele, and P.A. Fournier. 2002. Carbohydrate loading in human muscle: An improved 1-day protocol. *European Journal of Applied Physiology* 87, 3 (July):290–5.
T.J. Fairchild, S. Fletcher, P. Steele, C. Goodman, B. Dawson, and P.A. Fournier. 2002. Rapid carbohydrate loading after a short bout of near maximal-intensity exercise. *Medicine and Science in Sports and Exercise* 34, 6 (June):980–6.

5. B. Shepley, J.D. MacDougall, N. Cipriano, J.R. Sutton, M.A. Tarnopolsky, and G. Coates. 1992. Physiological effects of tapering in highly trained athletes. *Journal of Applied Physiology* 72, 2 (February):706–11.

6. J.A. Houmard, B.K. Scott, C.L. Justice, and T.C. Chenier. 1994. The effects of taper on performance in distance runners. *Medicine and Science in Sports and Exercise* 26, 5 (May):624–31.
J.P. Neary, Y.N. Bhambhani, and D.C. McKenzie. 2003. Effects of different stepwise reduction taper protocols on cycling performance. *Canadian Journal of Applied Physiology* 28, 4 (August):576–87.
I. Mujika, A. Goya, S. Padilla, A. Grijalba, E. Gorostiaga, and J. Ibanez. 2000. Physiological responses to a 6-d taper in middle-distance runners: Influence of training intensity and volume. *Medicine and Science in Sports and Exercise* 32, 2 (February):511–7.

7. Mujika et al. 2000.
J.P. Neary, T.P. Martin, D.C. Reid, R. Burnham, and H.A. Quinney. 1992. The effects of a reduced exercise duration taper programme on performance and muscle enzymes of endurance cyclists. *European Journal of Applied Physiology and Occupational Physiology* 65 (1):30–6.
J.P. Neary, T.P. Martin, and H.A. Quinney. 2003. Effects of taper on endurance cycling capacity and single muscle fiber properties. *Medicine and Science in Sports and Exercise* 35, 11 (November):1875–81.

TRAINING MYTHS 10

MYTH: I NEED MANY HOURS OF BASE MILES IN MY LEGS
TO PERFORM WELL.

The fact is that base miles may do more harm than good. Advocates of traditional training claim that several months of low-intensity miles are needed before athletes can start to work hard. This myth originates from the days before structured training when low-intensity training and high-intensity racing were the standard. As people "raced themselves into shape," they improved. Perhaps they improved because they started to do high-intensity exercise and didn't really need the base miles at all.

Endurance Explained

Endurance performance is a function of strong, well-fueled type I muscle fibers. It is true that only type I fibers are recruited during low-intensity base miles, however they are not used fully during long, low-intensity endurance rides. There is even some shrinkage of the muscle fibers, resulting in weaker endurance muscle.

To get stronger fibers, the fibers need to be larger. This happens with weight training and interval intensity. To get fibers that are capable of creating and using energy, you should perform certain workouts.

The important changes from the training effect are the increased number and function of mitochondria, the energy factories in the cells. They require enough carbohydrate and fat to be turned into energy.

Low-intensity endurance rides are the least productive way of inducing the desired training effect.

Workouts aimed at increasing energy production and blood supply are the priority in endurance training. Low-intensity endurance rides are the least productive way of inducing the desired training effect.

There is a point of diminishing returns with low-intensity endurance training. After about 2 hours of training, there is a decrease in the release of recovery hormones, and that decrease becomes large after 4 hours.

Release of recovery hormones increases with intensity and decreases with volume. Athletes need only 2–3 weeks of low-intensity endurance training. Although these weeks will not alone be responsible for endurance increases, they will prime the muscles for the release of recovery hormones during the riding and resistance exercises later.

The main benefit of low-intensity exercise is the depletion of stored carbohydrate fuel (muscle glycogen), but this comes at the expense of muscle protein, which is broken down to fuel the workout. Glycogen depletion occurs after several hours of riding, which is probably during the last hour of the workout. If timed right, this hour can be done first.

Glycogen depletion can occur in 1 hour of riding if the intensity is high enough. This hour must be shortly after waking up and before eating. In 1 hour, glycogen will be used up when you exercise at the lactate threshold heart rate. Keeping the workout to less than 1 hour will spare the muscles from breakdown.

Most important is the replenishment of muscle glycogen and protein after any workout. This is done with a meal of carbohydrate and protein in a 3:1 ratio (1 gram of carbohydrate and 0.3 grams of protein for every kilogram of body weight).

Endurance Recommendations

The pure endurance fibers can be trained in a variety of ways. To be sure they are all getting trained, you should be training at high to moderate intensity. Some suggested workouts are HIT, especially the 4- or 5-minute intervals at 80% of critical power; mitochondria biogenesis (Mito) workouts; low-carbohydrate diet for 3 days after Mito; and lipolysis (Lip).

As the training season progresses, you should add different types of workouts to increase intensity and replace traditional base miles. As previously mentioned, the training plan should start with a 2–3 week period of endurance training. This can be rides of 2–4 hours done 4 or 5 times a week.

One hour of glycogen depletion at 60% of critical power will elicit the endurance training effect.[1]

Perhaps the most significant way to increase endurance is by manipulating diet and exercise together. One such manipulation is to eat a high-fat diet (60–70% fat) for 5 days during endurance training. When you start to eat a high-carbohydrate diet again, the muscles will use an increasing amount of fat for fuel. Since fat can provide more energy for low-intensity exercise, this will allow you to go longer at lower intensities.

Another way to train the body to use fat is the lipolysis workout. Also best done first thing in the morning before eating, this 1-hour workout at a moderate or lactate threshold heart rate will increase the enzymes needed for fat usage. Again, it is important to eat afterward.

A low-carbohydrate diet for 3 days after glycogen depletion will also increase the endurance training effect more than glycogen depletion alone.[2] After the last day of a training block, eat low-carbohydrate food. When you return to high-carbohydrate food, the muscles will store the carbohydrate as glycogen more than they would have earlier. This will allow you to go longer and stronger.

MYTH: I NEED TO DO LOW-INTENSITY TRAINING TO LOSE WEIGHT.

Weight loss is a balance between calories you consume as food and calories you burn during exercise and daily activities. This principle is known as *energy balance*. In positive energy balance, you will gain weight; a negative energy balance results in weight loss. Several factors are important in energy balance. Food intake is the most important factor on the IN side of the scale, but there are several ways to expend calories OUT other than through low-intensity training. The equation for *energy balance* is:

$$\text{Food consumed} = \text{basal metabolic rate} + \text{exercise}$$

The OUT part of the energy-balance equation is made up of two parts (Figure 10.1): First is the basal metabolic rate, the amount of energy you use at rest; second is the energy expended during exercise. The basal metabolic rate increases with exercise and increased muscle mass.[3]

If the caloric intake is not sufficient for the caloric use (chronic negative energy balance), the basal metabolic rate will slow down. Diet and postexercise nutrition are important if weight loss is the goal.

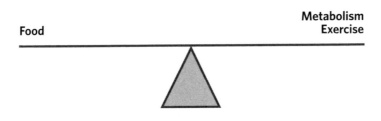

FIGURE 10.1 > The energy balance

Fat is maximally burned in a zone that corresponds to 65% of maximum heart rate. Exercise above this intensity also will lead to greater use of calories, although fat will not contribute to the increased fuel needs. If weight loss is the goal, high-intensity training is more efficient than low-intensity endurance to help you sustain a negative energy balance.

The hormones that increase lean body mass and the metabolic rate respond better to high-intensity training than they do to low-intensity endurance (Table 10.1), and more hormones promote weight loss and increased metabolic rate.

TABLE 10.1 Hormonal responses to training

HORMONE	HIGH-INTENSITY	LOW-INTENSITY
Thyroid hormone	↑	↓
Growth hormone	↑	↓
Testosterone	↑	↓

Weight loss is a balance between calories in and calories out. With high-intensity interval training and carefully planned fat-burning workouts, you can achieve weight-loss goals without compromising recovery. You do not need low-intensity exercise to increase your ability to lose weight.

MYTH: TAKING TIME OFF FROM TRAINING WILL HURT ME.

A popular fitness book from the 1980s stated that for every day you didn't train, you would require a week to regain the fitness you lost from that day off. This advice is nonsense.

Although probably few people believe that a single day off will affect performance dramatically, it is still a widely held notion that short periods of time off (detraining) will decrease. In fact, the opposite may be true: Short periods of time off may improve fitness. As shown in Table 10.2, the first reversal of the training effect occurs at 10 days of inactivity.

TABLE 10.2 Effects of inactivity on fitness

EFFECT	TIME	COMMENTS
Decreased capillary density[1]	2-3 weeks	
VO$_2$max decrease	3-8 weeks	
Oxidative fiber decrease	8 weeks	
Strength performance	4 weeks	
Muscle-fiber size: endurance athletes	Increases	
VO$_2$max decline[2]	Rapid, 2-4 weeks[3]	Remains greater than before training began[3]
VO$_2$max loss	4 weeks	
Decreased fat use, increased carbohydrate use	10 days	
Mitochondrial ATP production[4]	3 weeks	12-28% decrease[4]

Maximum training reduction with acceptable decrease in fitness

TRAINING REDUCTION	FITNESS KEPT
$\frac{2}{3}$ volume or frequency, maintain intensity[5]	No significant change in fitness[5]
7 weeks off[6]	Sprint/anaerobic power maintained[6]

NOTES:

1. I. Mujika and S. Padilla. 2001a. Muscular characteristics of detraining in humans. *Medicine and Science in Sports and Exercise* 33, 8 (August):1297-303.

2. I. Mujika and S. Padilla. 2001b. Cardiorespiratory and metabolic characteristics of detraining in humans. *Medicine and Science in Sports and Exercise* 33, 3 (March):413-21.

3. P.D. Neufer. 1989. The effect of detraining and reduced training on the physiological adaptations to aerobic exercise training. *Sports Medicine* 8, 5 (November):302-20.

4. R. Wibom, E. Hultman, M. Johansson, K. Matherei, D. Constantin-Teodosiu, and P.G. Schantz. 1992. Adaptation of mitochondrial ATP production in human skeletal muscle to endurance training and detraining. *Journal of Applied Physiology* 73, 5 (November):2004-10.

5. Neufer 1989.

6. M.T. Linossier, D. Dormois, C. Perier, J. Frey, A. Geyssant, and C. Denis. 1997. Enzyme adaptations of human skeletal muscle during bicycle short-sprint training and detraining. *Acta Physiologica Scandinavia* 161, 4 (December):439-45.

Although some effects can start to dissipate after only 4 days of complete in-activity, these declines can be prevented with previous strength training.

To perform well, you must stress your body. Repeated stress causes over-reaching. Stress must be followed by a period of recovery. If recovery is inade-quate, overreaching leads to overtraining. Most overreaching will improve after 3 days of rest, leaving you more fit than when you started.

To prepare adequately for a big event, it is even advisable to take extra time off for recovery. The main reason for structuring the training week into blocks of four days of work followed by three days of rest is to prepare you for the weekend races.

Another way of taking time off is the taper. During a taper, you will de-crease the number of intervals and total training volume by 50–85% over the 7–10 days preceding a big event. This might result in a training session with only one interval.

Regardless of how you take time off, think of it as a time to help your body recover from the stress of training.

Ignore the training myths regarding inactivity and you will find that you are better rested and stronger when you return to training.

SUMMARY ■ The benefits of low-intensity endurance training can be gained by replicating the useful parts of long rides while getting rid of the harmful parts.

■ When doing high-intensity training, the muscles will adapt to perform better over long distances than with low-intensity endurance.

■ Workouts aimed at increasing energy production and fat burning will improve endurance.

■ Weight loss is accomplished by using more energy than you take on as food.

■ High-intensity training uses more energy than low-intensity endurance.

■ Inactivity will not start to decrease fitness until approximately 7-10 days without exercise.

■ Time away from training helps the body to recover.

■ Using a taper is one way to take time off while improving fitness.

NOTES

1. N.K. Vollestad and P.C. Blom. 1985. Effect of varying exercise intensity on glycogen depletion in human muscle fibres. *Acta Physiologica Scandinavia* 125, 3 (November):395–405.

2. P.M. Garcia-Roves, D.H. Han, Z. Song, T.E. Jones, K.A. Hucker, and J.O. Holloszy. 2003. Prevention of glycogen supercompensation prolongs the increase in muscle GLUT4 after exercise. *American Journal of Physiology, Endocrinology, and Metabolism* 285, 4 (October):E729–36. Epub June 10, 2003.

3. W.J. Kraemer, N.A. Ratamess, and D.N. French. 2002. Resistance training for health and performance. *Current Sports Medicine Reports* 1, 3 (June):165–71.
J.R. Speakman and C. Selman. 2003. Physical activity and resting metabolic rate. *Proceedings of the Nutrition Society* 62, 3 (August):621–34.

RECIPES ‖

Poor nutrition alone won't ruin your fitness, nor will good nutrition by itself be sufficient to make you fit, but practicing proper nutritional habits can enhance your training. Proper nutrition before, during, and after training will enhance fuel-storage capacity, increase recovery, improve endurance, and increase the training effect. For all of these changes to occur, you should use several different categories of recipes: low-carbohydrate, mixed carbohydrate and protein, high-fat, and high-carbohydrate.

CARBOHYDRATE AND PROTEIN IN A 3-TO-1 RATIO

To optimize recovery after training or racing, you need to replenish your energy stores and rebuild muscle fibers. During recovery you get stronger, and you want to provide the muscles with the building blocks they need to improve. When you eat a large amount of carbohydrate both immediately after exercise and one hour later, you can stimulate your body to increase your energy reserves. Adding the right amount of protein will efficiently give your muscle cells the protein building blocks they need. This combination of carbohydrate and protein will enhance the secretion of recovery hormones.

TABLE: 11.1 Glycemic index of common foods

PERCENT	GRAIN	VEGETABLES, LEGUMES	FRUIT	BEVERAGE	SNACK
> 100	Baguette Rice Corn flakes Millet	Parsnips Baked potato Carrots Fava beans	Dates		Honey
90–100	Corn chips Wheat shred Crackers Barley	Rutabaga	Apricots		Mars Bar
80–89	Rye bread Rice Oatmeal	Beets Corn		Banana	
70–79	Raisin Bran Graham crackers Bread	French fries	Watermelon	Gatorade	Skittles Gatorade
60–69	Taco shells Shortbread Pumpernickel Pasta Couscous Bulgur	Peas Baked beans	Grapefruit Cantaloupe Raisins Pineapple Orange	Orange juice Pineapple juice Soft drinks	Twix Ice cream Sucrose
50–59	Whole wheat Pita bread Sourdough Ravioli	Lima beans Pinto beans Lentils	Banana Kiwi Mango Papaya Apple		Clif Bar Power Bar
40–49	Chickpeas Kidney beans			Milk Soy milk	Milk chocolate
30–39	Barley	Soy beans Peanuts Vegetables (nonroot)	Cheeries Plums		Fructose

HIGH-CARBOHYDRATE

The endurance athlete's diet should contain 60–70% carbohydrate. Most carbohydrate should come in the form of high-fiber, complex carbohydrates, such as whole grains. One way of defining carbohydrates is according to their value on the glycemic index. The glycemic index describes how quickly different foods are broken down into simple sugars. Carbohydrates that rank high on the

TABLE 11.2 Carbo-load sample daily menu (for 140-lb athlete)

Breakfast	
Bagel with 1 tbsp jelly	50
Orange juice 12 oz	45
Oatmeal ½ cup (pre-cooked measure) with ¼ cup raisins	58
Snack	
Banana	25
Yogurt drink	41
Orange juice (8 oz)	30
Lunch	
Pancakes	120
Orange juice (12 oz)	45
Snack	
Sorbet smoothie	60
Oatmeal ½ cup (pre-cooked measure) with ¼ cup raisins	58
Dinner	
Japanese Noodle Soup	100
Snack	
Muffin	36
Drink	
Carbohydrate-electrolyte beverage all day (3 water bottles)	108
Total	**776**

index (such as refined sugar and fruit sugars) are broken down into simple sugars quickly; low-glycemic-index carbohydrates take longer. Low-glycemic-index carbohydrates are the preferred energy source up to 2 hours before exercise and 2 hours after exercise. During and immediately after exercise, high-glycemic-index carbohydrates are preferred (Table 11.1).

To be sure you have enough energy stored away for an important race, you should eat a very high-carbohydrate diet for the 24 hours prior to the event. This increase in carbohydrate is known as *carbo-loading* (Table 11.2). To carbo-load fully, you should consume 12 grams of carbohydrate per kilogram of body weight in the 24 hours prior to an event. You can increase the storage of carbohydrate by first performing the carbo-load workout (CL) in Chapter 9.

HIGH-FAT

Usually, cyclists avoid high-fat diets. We are a weight-conscious group and tend to choose lower-fat foods. Not all fats are bad, however. The right choice of fat can spare carbohydrate stores for high-intensity activity.[1] High-fat diets for 5 days can increase the reliance upon fat as an energy source, even after the high-fat diet is stopped and the high-carbohydrate diet is started.

Choosing the right types of fat is important. Fats from vegetable sources (e.g., olive oil, avocado) are the best.[2] The fruit- and vegetable-based fats are called *unsaturated*. Eating unsaturated fats can actually jump-start fat breakdown and drive carbohydrate into the cells for storage during exercise.[3] Avoid *saturated* fats—fats that are solid at room temperature. These include fats from animal sources, partially hydrogenated oils, shortening, and palm oil (Table 11.3)

TABLE 11.3 Fat

GOOD FAT
Olive Oil
Avocado
Fish oil

BAD FAT
Partially hydrogenated vegetable oil
Saturated fat
Palm oil

LOW-CARBOHYDRATE

Increased endurance from the training effect is enhanced by depletion of muscle carbohydrate. Eating a low-carbohydrate diet for 3 days following a glycogen depletion workout (MITO) will result in an increased training effect.[4] For this dietary plan to work, it is imperative that the 3 days are absolute-rest days. Finish day 3 with a high-carbohydrate meal. A sample workout and menu plan might look like this:

	Day 1	Day 2	Day 3
Workout	Mito (in the a.m.)	off	off
Breakfast	Low-carb	Low-carb	Low-carb
Lunch	Low-carb	Low-carb	Low-carb
Dinner	Low-carb	Low-carb	High-carb

Using dietary periodization alone will not make you a star rider, but following proper dietary techniques can enhance your training.

See the appendix at the end of the chapter for high-carbohydrate, low-carbohydrate, and smoothie recipes.

NOTES

1. L.M. Burke and J.A. Hawley. 2002. Effects of short-term fat adaptation on metabolism and performance of prolonged exercise. *Medicine and Science in Sports and Exercise* 34, 9 (September):1492–8.

2. M. Alvizouri-Munoz, J. Carranza-Madrigal, J.E. Herrera-Abarca, F. Chavez-Carbajal, and J.L. Amezcua-Gastelum. 1992. Effects of avocado as a source of monounsaturated fatty acids on plasma lipid levels. *Archives of Medical Research* 23, 4 (Winter):163–7.

3. L.S. Piers, K.Z. Walker, R.M. Stoney, M.J. Soares, and K. O'Dea. 2002. The influence of the type of dietary fat on postprandial fat oxidation rates: monounsaturated (olive oil) vs saturated fat (cream). *International Journal of Obesity and Related Metabolic Disorders* 26, 6 (June):814–21.

L.S. Piers, K.Z. Walker, R.M. Stoney, M.J. Soares, and K. O'Dea. 2003. Substitution of saturated with monounsaturated fat in a 4-week diet affects body weight and composition of overweight and obese men. *British Journal of Nutrition* 90, 3 (September):717–27.

M. Uusitupa, U. Schwab, S. Makimattila, P. Karhapaa, E. Sarkkinen, H. Maliranta, J. Agren, and I. Penttila. 1994. Effects of two high-fat diets with different fatty acid compositions on glucose and lipid metabolism in healthy young women. *American Journal of Clinical Nutrition* 59, 6 (June):1310–6.

4. P.M. Garcia-Roves, D.H. Han, Z. Song, T.E. Jones, K.A. Hucker, and J.O. Holloszy. 2003. Prevention of glycogen supercompensation prolongs the increase in muscle GLUT4 after exercise. *American Journal of Physiology, Endocrinology, and Metabolism* 285, 4 (October):E729–36. Epub June 10, 2003.

CHAPTER 11 APPENDIX

Low-Carbohydrate Recipes

Frittata | Herb-crusted salmon | Scrambled eggs .
Steamed veggies with peanut sauce

Carbohydrates and Protein

5-minute chili | Potato and egg burrito | Black bean burritos
Curried eggs and peas | Pad Thai | Tofu and curry sauce
Mandarin tofu

High-Carbohydrate Recipes

Basic muffins | Noodle soup | Pancakes

Smoothies

Banana berry | Chocolate soy shake | Mango vanilla soy
Sorbet shake

LOW-CARBOHYDRATE RECIPES

Frittata

Amount	Ingredient	Fat (g)	Carb (g)	Protein (g)
1 cup	Egg whites (or egg substitute)	0	4	24
½	Medium onion, diced	0	12	2
¼ tsp	Garlic powder	0	0	0
¼ cup	Broccoli florets	0	5	3
¼ cup	Shredded cheese (optional)	18	1	14
	Total (2 servings) no cheese	**0**	**21**	**29**
	Total (2 servings) with cheese	**18**	**22**	**43**

■ Preheat oven to 350 degrees. Heat ovenproof skillet and spray with canola oil. Add onions to skillet and sauté until translucent. Add garlic powder and broccoli; sauté until the broccoli changes color. Add eggs (and cheese) and transfer to oven. Bake 10 minutes or until eggs are solid.

Herb-crusted salmon

Amount	Ingredient	Fat (g)	Carb (g)	Protein (g)
2 lbs	Salmon fillet	55	0	187
¼ cup	Chopped mint	0	0	0
¼ cup	Chopped basil	0	0	0
1 tsp	Mustard powder	0	0	0
½ tsp	Olive oil	7	0	0
	Salt	0	0	0
	Black pepper	0	0	0
	Total (6 servings)	**62**	**0**	**187**

■ Preheat oven to 425 degrees. Wash fish and place in baking dish. Salt and pepper fish to taste. Mix mint, basil, and mustard in a bowl and slowly add olive oil until the chopped herbs form a paste. Spread herb-and-oil mixture over fish. Bake 20 minutes or until fish is cooked through and flakes when broken with a fork.

Scrambled eggs

Scrambled eggs are a satisfying, low-carbohydrate meal.

Amount	Ingredient	Fat (g)	Carb (g)	Protein (g)
½ cup	Egg whites (or egg substitute)	0	2	12
	Salt and pepper to taste	0	0	0
1 spray	Canola oil	0	0	0
	Total (1 serving)	**0**	**2**	**12**

■ Heat a skillet and spray oil on the bottom. Gently whisk eggs with a fork and pour into skillet. Add salt and pepper. As the eggs begin to harden, push the edges toward the center with a spatula. Continue to cook until no more liquid remains in pan.

Steamed veggies with peanut sauce

Amount	Ingredient	Fat (g)	Carb (g)	Protein (g)
1 cup	Broccoli florets	0	9	5
1	Carrots, chopped	0	7	1
1 can	Baby corn	0	7	3.5
6 tbsp	Peanut butter	48	18	30
⅓ cup	Vegetable broth	0	0	0
1	Scallion, chopped	0	0	0
2 tbsp	Soy sauce	0	0	0
1 tsp	Mustard	0	0	0
1-2 cloves	Garlic, minced	0	0	0
1 tsp	Fresh grated ginger	0	0	0
	Total (2-3 servings)	**48**	**41**	**39.5**

■ Steam vegetables. Combine the remaining ingredients in a small pot over low heat. You may need to add more broth if the sauce becomes too thick.

CARBOHYDRATES AND PROTEIN

5-minute chili

Amount	Ingredient	Fat (g)	Carb (g)	Protein (g)
1 can (15-20 oz)	Kidney, pinto, or black beans	1	49	15
2 jars (16 oz)	Salsa	0	6	0
1 lb	Soy "ground meat"	1	7	11
1	Medium onion, chopped	0	12	2
1	Small summer squash, chopped	0	3	1
1 spray	Canola oil	0	0	0
½ cup	Rice, cooked	1	74	6
	Total (Serves 3-4)	**3**	**151**	**35**

■ Cook rice according to package directions. Heat saucepan and spray oil on bottom of pan. Sauté onions until translucent. Add summer squash and cook until tender. Sauté soy meat until it crumbles. Add beans and salsa and cook until heated through. Serve over rice.

Potato and egg burrito

Amount	Ingredient	Fat (g)	Carb (g)	Protein (g)
2	Potatoes, peeled and cubed	0	36	4
1	Onion, chopped	0	10	1
2 cloves	Garlic, chopped	0	0	0
½	Red pepper, sliced	0	3	1
4	Egg whites	0	4	24
4	Flour tortillas	12	88	12
1 spray	Olive oil	0	0	0
	Total (2 servings)	**12**	**141**	**42**

■ Steam or boil cubed potatoes until tender. Spray oil on the bottom of a heated skillet. Add garlic and onions and sauté until translucent. Add pepper and potatoes; cook until tender. Push the potatoes to the sides of the pan and add eggs to the center of the pan. Drag a spatula across the cooking eggs to create chunks of eggs. Continue to cook until liquid has evaporated. Spoon mixture into tortillas and roll up.

Black bean burritos

Beans and rice have a full complement of amino acids, the building blocks of protein. The combination is low in fat and high in carbohydrate content. Different brands of tortillas have different carbohydrate and fat contents. Avoid lard and hydrogenated oils in the tortillas that you buy.

Amount	Ingredient	Fat (g)	Carb (g)	Protein (g)
1 can (20 oz)	Black beans	0	20	7
1 cup	Frozen corn	0	34	5
4 cloves	Garlic	0	0	0
½ tbsp	Olive oil	7	0	0
¼ tsp	Cayenne pepper	0	0	0
½ tsp	Oregano	0	0	0
1 tsp	Cumin	0	0	0
1 dash	Liquid smoke	0	0	0
1 dash	Hot pepper sauce	0	0	0
1 small	Onion, chopped	0	8	1
½	Red pepper, chopped	0	4	1
1 cup	Brown rice	0	50	5
6	Tortillas	18	192	24
	Total (3 servings)	**25**	**308**	**43**

- Heat oil; fry garlic until brown. Add onion and pepper, and sauté until translucent. Add spices and sauté until fragrant. Add corn, beans, liquid smoke, and pepper sauce and cook on medium heat. In a separate pot, cook rice with 1 ¼ cup water and a pinch of cumin.

- Heat tortillas in a microwave or a warm pan. Place tortillas flat on a plate and spoon rice and beans into the center. Fold the edge closest to you over the beans and rice, then fold in the sides and continue rolling.

Curried eggs and peas

This recipe can be used as a low-carbohydrate meal when served without rice and peas.

Amount	Ingredient	Fat (g)	Carb (g)	Protein (g)
1 cup (8 oz)	Plain nonfat yogurt	4	35	8
2 tsp	Flour	0	5	0
1 spray	Cooking spray	0	0	0
1 package (10 oz)	Frozen peas	0	23	8
1 cup	Thinly sliced onions	0	12	2
2 tsp	Curry powder	0	0	0
6	Hard-cooked egg whites	0	0	24
	Total without rice	**4**	**75**	**42**
1 cup	Cooked rice	1	149	12
	Total with rice (3 servings)	**5**	**224**	**54**

■ Hard-cook eggs by placing eggs in single layer in saucepan. Add enough tap water to come at least 1 inch above eggs. Cover. Quickly bring just to boiling. Turn off heat. If necessary, remove pan from burner to prevent further boiling. Let eggs stand, covered, in the hot water, 15 minutes for large eggs (about 18 minutes for extra large and about 12 minutes for medium). After cooking time, run cold water over eggs or place them in ice water until completely cooled.

■ To remove shell: Crackle shell by tapping gently all over. Roll egg between hands to loosen shell. Then peel, starting at large end. Hold egg under running cold water or dip in bowl of water to help ease off shell.

■ In small bowl, stir together yogurt and flour. Set aside.

■ Evenly coat 10-inch omelet pan or skillet with spray. Over low heat, cook peas, onions, and curry powder, covered, until onions are tender and peas are heated through, about 7 to 10 minutes. Stir in reserved yogurt mixture. Gently stir in eggs. Cook, stirring occasionally, until heated through.

■ For each serving, spoon ¾ cup egg mixture over rice.

Pad Thai

Amount	Ingredient	Fat (g)	Carb (g)	Protein (g)
2 tbsp	Fish sauce*	0	0	0
¼ cup	Soy sauce*	0	0	0
¼ cup	Rice vinegar*	0	0	0
2 tsp	Tamarind paste (available at Asian markets)	1	20	0
¼ cup	Sugar	0	50	0
8 cloves	Garlic, chopped	0	0	0
14-16 oz	Rice noodles	0	50	0
1 tbsp	Vegetable or peanut oil	14	0	0
1 lb	Firm tofu, cut in small cubes	5	1	13
1 cup	Summer squash, chopped	0	8	2
1 ½ cup	Broccoli	0	14	7
1 cup	Snow peas	0	8	3
½ cup	Egg whites (or egg substitute)	0	2	12
2	Scallions, chopped	0	0	0
	Total (4 servings)	**20**	**153**	**37**

■ Assemble fish sauce, soy sauce, rice vinegar, sugar, and tamarind paste in a bowl; set aside. Boil water in a pot and cook noodles 2 minutes; strain and set aside. In a separate wok or pan, sauté garlic in oil until brown, add tofu, and sauté 3 minutes. Add vegetables and cook until tender. Add noodles and sauce and mix thoroughly.

■ If using the eggs, push the noodles to the side of the wok and scramble the eggs until solid, then mix in with the noodles and vegetables rather than let the eggs coat the noodles.

*NOT A SIGNIFICANT SOURCE OF CALORIES FROM FAT OR CARBOHYDRATE.

Tofu and curry sauce

This recipe can be a stand-alone dish without the peas for a low-carbohydrate meal, or can be served over noodles or rice to boost the carbohydrate content. The fat comes from unsaturated sources and is a great source of fuel for endurance at submaximal intensity.

Amount	Ingredient	Fat (g)	Carb (g)	Protein (g)
2 tsp	Canola oil	10	0	0
½ large	Yellow onion, chopped	0	12	2
3 cloves	Chopped garlic	0	1	0
1	Red pepper, chopped	0	4	1
1 tsp	Grated ginger	0	0	0
1 lb	Extra-firm tofu, cubed	25	5	65
1 tbsp	Curry powder	0	0	0
½ tsp	Ground coriander	0	0	0
½ tsp	Salt	0	0	0
¼ tsp	Ground black pepper	0	0	0
¾ cup	Vegetable broth	0	0	0
¾ cup	Soy milk	2	9	6
1 cup	Peas	0	18	8
2 tbsp	Arrowroot			
	Total (3–4 servings)	**37**	**49**	**82**

■ Heat oil in pan. Sauté onion, garlic, and ginger until onions are translucent. Add pepper, tofu, and peas. Add spices and stir until tofu is coated. Dissolve arrowroot in broth. Add soy milk and arrowroot/broth mixture to pan and cook until sauce thickens. Serve over rice or noodles.

Mandarin tofu

Amount	Ingredient	Fat (g)	Carb (g)	Protein (g)
2 tsp	Sesame oil	10	0	0
1 lb	Firm tofu cut into strips	3	2	7
1/4 tsp	Salt	0	0	0
1/4 tsp	Ground black pepper	0	0	0
2 cups (or 2 11-oz cans)	Mandarin oranges, rinsed	0	33	2
1	Red pepper, seeded and diced	0	4	1
1 tbsp	Hoisin sauce	0	11	1
1/4 cup	Scallions, chopped	0	0	0
1 cup	Rice	1	149	12
	Total (3-4 servings)	**14**	**199**	**23**

▪ Prepare rice. Heat oil in wok. Add tofu and sauté until starting to brown. Add salt and ground pepper to tofu. Add mandarins, red pepper, and hoisin sauce. Bring to a simmer. Reduce heat to low and cook until sauce thickens and oranges break down.

HIGH-CARBOHYDRATE RECIPES

Basic muffins (makes ½ dozen)

These muffins are good as a stand-alone snack, but can have the carbohydrate content further increased by adding fruit and nuts.

Amount	Ingredient	Fat (g)	Carb (g)	Protein (g)
2 cups	Flour	0	176	12
½ cup	Sugar	0	100	0
2 tsp	Baking powder	0	2	0
1 tsp	Baking soda	0	0	0
1 cup + 1 tbsp	Vanilla yogurt	2	23	4
½ cup	Soy milk	2	4	4
2 tbsp	Arrowroot	0	0	0
1 tbsp	Corn oil	14	0	0
	Recipe total	**18**	**305**	**20**

- Preheat oven to 350 degrees. Combine the flour, sugar, baking powder, and baking soda in a mixing bowl and stir together. Make a well in the center of the flour mixture and pour in the remaining ingredients. Stir together until well blended, but don't overbeat. The batter should be medium-thick. If it seems too stiff or dry, add a small amount of additional milk.

- Stir in the additional ingredient(s) of your choice (see variations), then divide the batter among 6 oiled or foil-lined muffin tins. Bake 20 minutes, or until the tops of the muffins are golden and a toothpick inserted into the center of one comes out clean. Let cool until just warm to the touch, then transfer muffins to a plate. When muffins are completely cooled, store in an airtight container.

Muffin variations:

1. Raisin or raisin-nut: Add 1 cup raisins or ¾ cup raisins plus ¼ cup finely chopped walnuts, plus ½ teaspoon of cinnamon.

2. Blueberry: Add 1 cup fresh or frozen blueberries.

3. Strawberry: Add 1 cup very sweet chopped fresh or frozen strawberries.

4. Apple: Add 1 cup finely chopped apple, and if you'd like, ¼ cup raisins or chopped walnuts and 1 teaspoon of cinnamon.

5. Chocolate chip: Add ¾ to 1 cup semisweet chocolate chips or minichips.

6. Cocoa: Add ½ cup sweetened chocolate milk powder and reduce the sugar to ¼ cup. You can add nuts or raisins to these as well.

7. Pear and golden raisin: Add ½ cup each finely chopped ripe pear and golden raisins.

8. Dried Fruit: Add ⅔ cup finely chopped mixed dried fruits, such as apricots, apples, dates, mangoes, and papaya.

9. Banana: Add 1 cup chopped banana or ½ cup chopped banana combined with ½ cup semisweet chocolate minichips.

Noodle soup

Amount	Ingredient	Fat (g)	Carb (g)	Protein (g)
7 cups	Water	0	0	0
6 inch strip	Kombu*	0	0	0
1 oz (2 cups unpacked)	Bonito flakes*	0	0	0
½ cup	Soy Sauce	0	8	0
3 tbsp	Mirin (Sweet Japanese cooking wine)	0	21	0
2	Carrots, sliced	0	13	0
2	Scallions, minced	0	0	0
½ pound	Tofu, cut in ½ inch cubes	15	3	25
1 pound	Udon noodles	4	320	70
	Total (3 servings)	**19**	**365**	**95**

- Cook noodles according to package directions, set aside.
- Add kombu and water and bring to a boil.
- Place bonito flakes in a tea strainer and add to pot; simmer for 3 minutes.
- Add soy sauce and mirin; simmer for 5 minutes.
- Remove Kombu.
- Add carrots and tofu, cover and simmer for 5 minutes.
- Place cooked noodles in soup bowls and cover with broth.
- Sprinkle scallions over the top of each bowl.

* AVAILABLE IN ASIAN MARKETS

Pancakes

Amount	Ingredient	Fat (g)	Carb (g)	Protein (g)
1 cup	Flour	1	76	7
1 tsp	Applesauce	0	0.6	0
2 tsp	Baking powder	0	1	0
¼ cup	Egg white	0	1	6
1 cup	Vanilla soy milk	4	8	7
1 tsp	Vanilla extract	0	0	0
¼ tsp	Salt	0	0	0
1 cup	Blueberries	1	20	1
¼ cup	Maple syrup	0	128	0
1 cup	Strawberries	1	10	1
	Total (2–3 servings)	**7**	**245**	**22**

■ Heat the strawberries in maple syrup on low heat.

■ Combine all other ingredients in a blender to make a smooth batter.

■ Preheat a nonstick pan and spray with oil. Use a paper towel to spread the oil over the pan. Spoon batter into pan to make 3- to 4-inch pancakes. When bubbles appear on the pancakes, add blueberries and flip. Serve with warm maple-strawberry syrup.

SMOOTHIES

Banana berry

Amount	Ingredient	Fat (g)	Carb (g)	Protein (g)
1	Frozen banana	0	25	0
10 oz (1/2 can)	Canned pineapple	0	37	0
½ cup	Frozen berries	0	5	1
1 cup	Orange Juice	0	30	0
1 scoop	Protein Powder	5	0	20
	Total (1 serving)	**5**	**97**	**21**

■ Prepare frozen bananas ahead of time by peeling and placing in a plastic bag before freezing.

■ Blend ingredients.

Chocolate soy shake

Amount	Ingredient	Fat (g)	Carb (g)	Protein (g)
1 cup	Chocolate Soy Milk	3.5	23	5
1 cup	Vanilla or Plain Yogurt	3	22	5
1	Frozen banana	0	25	0
1 scoop	Protein Powder	1	70	14
	Total (1 serving)	**7.5**	**140**	**24**

■ Blend ingredients until smooth.

Mango vanilla soy

Amount	Ingredient	Fat (g)	Carb (g)	Protein (g)
1 cup (2 handfulls)	Frozen mango	0	63	3
1 cup	Vanilla soy milk	3.5	10	6
½ cup	Plain or vanilla yogurt	1.5	11	3
½ scoop	Protein powder		0	10
	Total (1 serving)	**5**	**84**	**19**

■ Blend ingredients together. This recipe is inspired by the Mango Lassi, a popular drink in South Asia.

Sorbet shake

Amount	Ingredient	Fat (g)	Carb (g)	Protein (g)
1 cup	Lemon sorbet	0	40	0
1 cup	Frozen raspberries or strawberries	1	20	3
1 cup	Seltzer	0	0	0
20g	Protein powder	5	0	20
	Total (1 serving)	**6**	**60**	**23**

■ Blend all ingredients until smooth. Add seltzer as needed for desired consistency.

TRAINING PLANS 12

Whether you have been reading this book from its beginning or sampling random pages, by now you have learned some of the exercise and sport science that should help you shape and define your training.

Base miles, although widely adopted by many athletes, need not consume several months of your time to be effective. Other types of workouts can replace base miles while increasing the fitness you need and allowing for proper recovery.

Intensity, whether achieved through weight training or interval training, will cause a transformation of the powerful and versatile type IIa muscle fibers. Resistance training will increase the size and power of the fibers; interval training will increase their function. Combined, these two training modalities will generate muscle that can work harder and longer.

These changes will improve performance, but they occur during recovery from exercise. Each chapter in this book tells you how to train with the purpose of improved recovery in mind. Recovery is as important as the specific training techniques and is an important part of the overall training plan.

THE TRAINING PHASES

Priming Phase

The priming phase is a short, low-intensity period that will set you up for better recovery later. Three weeks of low to moderate intensity will teach your muscles to use energy better. More important, this brief priming phase will lead to increased secretion of recovery hormones during subsequent exercise.

During this phase, you may choose lipolysis, mitochondrial biogenesis, and short to moderate endurance workouts (Table 12.1). Grouping the workout days and rest days will be helpful for recovery. I prefer a 4-day work block followed by a 3-day rest block. Nutrition during the priming phase should consist of high-carbohydrate, low-fat meals. To maximize the secretion of recovery hormones, avoid fat and simple sugars before bed.

TABLE 12.1 Priming workouts

WORKOUTS
Lipolysis 1 (Lip1)
Lipolysis 2 (Lip2)
Mitochondrial biogenesis 1 (Mito1)
Mitochondrial biogenesis 2 (Mito2)
Low-intensity endurance

A sample training week might look like this:

Day	Workout
Saturday	Endurance (2–4 hours, zone 3)
Sunday	Lip1 + 2 hours low-intensity endurance
Monday	Lip2
Tuesday	Mito1
Wednesday	Off
Thursday	Off
Friday	Off

You will notice that a longer ride on Sunday is not done solely by increasing volume but also by adding volume to a lipolysis ride. By using this combination, you are getting the most out of your training hours without decreasing your ability to recover. This leaves you able to train again the next day while maintaining intensity.

The 3-day rest period should be a break from exercise but not from training. This is the time to focus on sleep and nutrition. Continue to eat well and be sure you are getting adequate sleep (see "Sleep and recovery"). If you are still tired when you wake up, you likely are not getting enough sleep.

During the priming phase, it is useful to perform the initial tests that will serve as baselines for your fitness later. As you begin your training, establish your heart rate training zones with a modified Conconi test. Also try to determine your cadence zones with the

TABLE 12.2 Priming volume

CATEGORY	DAILY VOLUME
Pro, elite	4 hours
2,3, sport	2.5-4 hours
4,5, beginner	2.5 hours
Recreational	2-2.5 hours

Sleep and recovery

Much of the repair and recovery that you need after exercise occurs while you are sleeping. This is largely the result of two hormones that are secreted during sleep. To determine if you are getting enough sleep, evaluate how you feel in the morning. If you are waking up feeling tired, you probably haven't slept enough.

One common mistake people make is trying to "catch up" on lost sleep. Your body needs to become adjusted to a fixed schedule, and the closer you stick to that schedule, the better rested you will feel.

One strategy for finding a sleep schedule that is right for you is to go to bed 30 minutes earlier each night until you awake refreshed. Also, try to condition yourself for sleep by getting into a fixed routine before bed, perhaps reading a book or browsing the Internet. These external clues, called zeitgeibers, will help you to fall asleep more easily.

ideal-cadence test. At the start of the final week, perform the critical-power test. Now that you are primed, you are ready to start adding intensity.

Hypertrophy Phase

The goal during the hypertrophy phase is to increase muscle size, which will increase muscle strength. The increase in muscle size is accomplished mainly with resistance training of high volume and low loads. Although the muscles will increase in size and force production, aerobic capacity can decrease because the number of mitochondria does not increase as well. Mitochondrial biogenesis and lipolysis workouts can be done on the days in between the lifting, but be aware that your legs may feel sore and weak. Keep the cadence high when riding during the hypertrophy phase (Table 12.3).

TABLE 12.3 Hypertrophy-phase workouts

RESISTANCE	CYCLING
10-12 reps, 3-4 sets of the following:	Lip1
Leg press x 4 weeks	Lip2
Squat x 4 weeks	Mito1
	Mito2
	Mito3
Triple push-up x 4 weeks	
Pull-up or seated row x 4 weeks	
Core strength	
Back extension	
Stability-ball crunch	
Weighted leg raise	

Note in this sample of the hypertrophy phase that there is limited use of the leg-extension and leg-curl exercises. Cyclists want to gain strength without gaining bulk. By limiting the amount of single-joint resistance exercises, you should be able to reduce the amount of added bulk.

	Weeks 1–2	Weeks 3–4
Saturday	Resistance (single and multijoint)	Resistance (multijoint only)
Sunday	Lip (1 or 2)	Lip (1 or 2)
Monday	Resistance (single and multijoint)	Resistance (multijoint only)
Tuesday	Lip (1 or 2)	Lip (1 or 2)
Wednesday	Resistance (single and multijoint)	Resistance (multijoint only)
Thursday	Off	Off
Friday	Off	Off

If you need to develop more pedaling force, you may continue the hypertrophy phase for up to 6 weeks by repeating weeks 3–4 for another 1–2 weeks. The benefits of doing this include increased strength, but this may come at the expense of decreased cycling-specific exercise.

Strength Phase

During the strength phase, you will build upon the hypertrophy phase by increasing training intensity and developing mitochondria. You may find that riding during the strength phase will be less difficult than during the hypertrophy phase. Now that the muscle fibers are increased in size, they will learn to handle an increased load. During the strength phase (Table 12.4), you will begin to resupply the muscles with energy from mitochondria and capillary growth.

TABLE 12.4 Strength-phase workouts

RESISTANCE	CYCLING
8, 6, 4 reps depending upon the day, 4 sets	Mito1
Leg press	Mito2
Squat	Mito3
10-12 reps, 4 sets	
Triple push-up or bench press	
Pull-up or seated row	

These workouts are arranged similarly to those in the hypertrophy phase, but the intensity is greater in the strength phase. Another feature unique to the strength phase is the application of daily undulating periodization (DUP) to the resistance component of the training. DUP has been shown to increase strength more than standard weight increases can. To increase strength, you will vary the amount of weight lifted based upon the day of the week. On day 1, lift as much as you can for 8 reps. On day 2, use enough weight to lift 6 reps. On day 3, perform 4 reps with an appropriate weight. The next week, you will start with 8 reps again. Because you are stressing your body and then backing down, you will find that each time you return to lifting your 8 rep maximum, you will feel that the weight is light and that you will be able to increase the weight easily.

During the strength phase, sprinters and general riders will follow different lifting programs. Because sprinters seek maximum power, they will do a longer strength phase with a switch to 6, 4, and 2 reps for the last week of it and then add another week of the same.

For general riders, the sample week for all weeks of this phase will look like the plan on the next page.

Day	Weeks 1–4
Saturday	8 reps max
Sunday	Mito
Monday	6 reps max
Tuesday	Mito
Wednesday	4 reps max
Thursday	Off
Friday	Off

Here are sample weeks for sprinters:

Day	Weeks 1–3	Weeks 4–5
Saturday	8 reps max	6 reps max
Sunday	Mito	Mito
Monday	6 reps max	4 reps max
Tuesday	Mito	Mito
Wednesday	4 reps max	2 reps max
Thursday	Off	Off
Friday	Off	Off

The end of the strength phase marks the end of the intense lifting, and now it is time for full-blown bicycling.

Power Phase

You are now ready to bring together the larger, stronger muscles you have developed. This involves producing large forces quickly. Force production is *strength,* but force production over a short time is *power.* Some trainers advocate developing power in the weight room by moving low weight at a fast velocity that is specific to motions used in cycling. Others have found that moving weight at this speed results in the need to slow the movement at the end of the range of motion, which limits the utility of this type of lifting. I believe that if you want to have sport-specific movements, you should be doing sport-specific exercise. This is done on the bicycle with interval intensity.

High-intensity training

You will want to develop power in three different types of situations: long-, medium-, and short-duration efforts. The use of high-intensity training (HIT) will promote the forces you need by developing all of the muscle fibers used during each type of effort.

Chapter 6 presented three types of HIT intervals to perform. The basic HIT workout uses daily undulating periodization and short intervals to build strength and power on the bike. The next phase uses longer intervals over long, sustained intensity in order to build strength. To develop the forceful contractions needed during sprinting efforts, postactivation potentiation (PAP) is used as an effective tool for generating greater power. Continuously testing your critical power will allow you to track your changes and plateaus and will help you determine when to switch from one type of interval to the other.

Arranging the testing and intervals will give you this sample schedule:

	Weeks 1, 3, 5	Weeks 2, 4, 6 (sprinter)	Weeks 2, 4, 6 (general)
Saturday	Critical-power test + HIT	HIT	Mito
Sunday	HIT	HIT (or PAP)	HIT
Monday	HIT	HIT	Mito
Tuesday	HIT	HIT (or PAP)	HIT
Wednesday	Off	Off	Off
Thursday	Off	Off	Off
Friday	Off	Off	Off

Sustained power and muscle endurance (SPAM)

As you get stronger and progress, your critical power should increase with repeat testing. When retesting no longer yields increased critical power or six weeks have elapsed, the intervals are lengthened to develop sustained power. At this time, the training week will fit one of these patterns:

	Weeks 1–4	Alternate Weeks 1–4	Sprinters
Saturday	SPAM	SPAM	SPAM
Sunday	HIT	SPAM	PAP
Monday	SPAM	SPAM	SPAM
Tuesday	HIT	SPAM	PAP
Wednesday	Off	Off	Off
Thursday	Off	Off	Off
Friday	Off	Off	Off

When you can perform the intervals easily, it is time to increase power. Unlike the HIT intervals, SPAM intervals are increased linearly—that is, the power is increased only from day to day without the fluctuations. Linear periodization has been shown to increase endurance. You can either increase the interval power by 10 watts or retest your critical power to determine by how much you should increase the intervals.

Explosive power

Sprinters or those who are trying to develop explosive force might opt to use postactivation potentiation (PAP). PAP is a 15-second sprint interval following a maximal isometric contraction. The maximal contraction will stimulate increased force production. PAP workouts can be substituted for HIT intervals in the last two weeks of HIT.

THE RACING SEASON

Racing is a series of high-intensity intervals alternating with sustained power intervals in rapid succession. The only difference lies in the lack of structure in racing for recovery and intervals. Because of the similarity in intensity, it is easy to replace a training day with a race day. If you continue the same structure, your week could look like this, depending upon which day you race.

Saturday	Race *(low-priority)*	Carbo-load	Race *(high- or low-priority)*
Sunday	Race *(low-priority)*	Race *(high-priority)*	HIT or SPAM
Monday	HIT or SPAM	HIT or SPAM	HIT or SPAM
Tuesday	HIT or SPAM	HIT or SPAM	HIT or SPAM
Wednesday	Off	Off	Off
Thursday	Off	Off	Off
Friday	Off	Off	Off

If a particular race leaves you especially tired, you can shorten the training week to 3 days by either resting the day afterward or training only for 1 or 2 days, depending upon whether you raced for 1 or 2 days. That schedule produces a total of 3 days on and 4 days off.

During the racing season, it is a good idea to reduce the number of intervals by half to two-thirds while maintaining intensity; this is especially true the week before a high-priority race.

TIMING THE PLAN

Now that you have a basic idea of how to train, the next step is to plan the program so that you achieve your highest level of fitness for your most important events. The time of maximum fitness will follow the SPAM workouts and should last 4 to 6 weeks. If you have other important races that do not fall within that window, you can plan to rest and increase fitness again later in the season. For instance, if you want to do well at one event in April and another in August, you should plan for two fitness peaks. As long as the events are separated by 6–8 weeks, you have enough time to rest and increase your fitness for the second event.

Alternatively, you can try to be fit for an entire season. If you will be racing for only a short period of time (6–8 weeks), plan to peak once during the season and aim to maintain your fitness throughout the entire season.

Either way, you should arrive at your first major race with the majority of the HIT and SPAM work done. But even if you don't have the bulk of the HIT or SPAM phases completed you should not forgo racing; in fact, racing is the best way to train for cycling competition. Following the schedules previously laid out will ensure that you have adequate recovery.

After you have determined when you want to be most fit, count backward a certain number of weeks to determine when you must begin training to peak at the correct time (Table 12.5). The length of time you need to reach your fitness goals will depend upon your training history and experience.

Knowing how long you need to develop peak fitness will allow you to plan your training program. Allow for some flexibility in case of illness, injury, or other circumstances that result in detraining time.

TABLE 12.5 Weeks until peak fitness

PHASE	BEGINNER	EXPERIENCED
Priming	3-4 weeks	3 weeks
Hypertrophy	3-4 weeks	3 weeks
Strength	4-6 weeks	4-6 weeks
HIT	4-6 weeks	2-6 weeks
SPAM	6-8 weeks	4-6 weeks
Rest	1 week	1 week
Total	21-29 weeks	17-25 weeks

In order to be ready to race, it is important to have the final "taper" week completed. This readiness will allow you to race after recovery and enjoy all of the training benefits you will have worked so hard to obtain.

Taper Phase

Training hard is difficult, demanding work. In order for the body to rest and recover, you must decrease volume and maintain intensity. This is called the "taper" stage. A taper can last 3–10 days, but one week should be sufficient.

When tapering, decrease the volume by 50–85%. Instead of doing 8 reps of a particular exercise, do 3–4 reps but maintain the level of power output.

There are two times to taper: one before a high-priority race and another before a fitness peak. The taper before a race should occur the week before the event.

Second Peak

To achieve a second peak, you first need to create a valley. This is done by decreasing volume while maintaining intensity. The training valley should last up to 2 weeks and end 4 weeks before the second peak. The valley is essentially a long taper that will allow you to recover from racing and training shortly before you increase toward the second peak.

Cyclists have not shown a decline in fitness by decreasing both training volume and intensity for 3 weeks, so it is unlikely that a decrease in volume will lead to a decrease in fitness, especially if intensity is maintained.[1]

NOTES

1. G.J. Rietjens, H.A. Keizer, H. Kuipers, and W.H. Saris. 2001. A reduction in training volume and intensity for 21 days does not impair performance in cyclists. *British Journal of Sports Medicine* 35, 6 (December):431–4.

CHAPTER 12 APPENDIX

Beginner Training Plan

Sprinter Training Plan

General Training Plan

Beginner training plan

The following training plan maps out a 24-week schedule. You will find the descriptions of the workouts specified in Chapter 9. On days without a specified resistance or bike workout, you should rest. Some of the rest periods are noted in the training plans below. In weeks 13-15, the Bike column follows a 3 days on/3 days off pattern, and the Alternate Bike column follows a 3 days on/4 days off pattern. Continue this pattern for the final 10 days of the training block.

WEEK	DAY	RESISTANCE	BIKE	ALTERNATE BIKE
	Saturday		LIP	
	Sunday		LIP	
	Monday		LIP	
1	Tuesday			
	Wednesday			
	Thursday		REST	
	Friday			
	Saturday		LIT 1.5 hr	MITO 1.5 hr
	Sunday		LIT 2 hr	MITO 2 hr
	Monday		MITO	LIP
2	Tuesday		MITO	LIP
	Wednesday			
	Thursday		REST	
	Friday			
	Saturday		MITO 2.5 hr	
	Sunday		MITO 2.5 hr	
	Monday		LIP	LIP +1 hr MITO
3-4	Tuesday		LIP	LIP + 1 hr MITO
	Wednesday			
	Thursday		REST	
	Friday			
	Saturday	Hypert		
	Sunday		LIP, MITO	
	Monday	Hypert		
5-8	Tuesday		LIP, MITO	
	Wednesday	Hypert		
	Thursday			
	Friday		REST	

WEEK	DAY	RESISTANCE	BIKE	ALTERNATE BIKE
	Saturday	Strength		
	Sunday		MITO	
	Monday	Strength		
9–12	Tuesday		MITO	
	Wednesday	Strength		
	Thursday			
	Friday		REST	
	Saturday		HIT	HIT
	Sunday		HIT	HIT
	Monday		HIT	HIT
	Tuesday			HIT
	Wednesday			
13–15	Thursday			
	Friday		HIT	
	Saturday		HIT	HIT
	Sunday		HIT	HIT
	Monday			HIT
	Tuesday			HIT
	Saturday		HIT	
	Sunday		SPAM	
	Monday		HIT	
16–20	Tuesday		SPAM	
	Wednesday			
	Thursday		REST	
	Friday			
	Saturday		HIT	Race
	Sunday		PAP	Race
	Monday		SPAM	PAP or HIT
21–24	Tuesday		PAP	SPAM
	Wednesday			
	Thursday		REST	
	Friday			

Sprinter training plan

The following training plan maps out a 26-week schedule. You will find the descriptions of the workouts specified in Chapter 9.

WEEK	DAY	RESISTANCE	BIKE	ALTERNATE BIKE
1-3	Saturday		MITO, LIP	
	Sunday		MITO, LIP	
	Monday		MITO, LIP	
	Tuesday		MITO, LIP	
	Wednesday		MITO, LIP	
	Thursday		REST	
	Friday			
4-9	Saturday	Hypertrophy		
	Sunday		LIP	
	Monday	Hypertrophy		
	Tuesday		LIP	
	Wednesday	Hypertrophy		
	Thursday		REST	
	Friday			
10-15	Saturday	Strength		
	Sunday		MITO, LIP	
	Monday	Strength		
	Tuesday		MITO, LIP	
	Wednesday	Strength		
	Thursday		REST	
	Friday			

WEEK	DAY	RESISTANCE	BIKE		ALTERNATE BIKE
	Saturday		HIT	or	HIT or Training Race
	Sunday		PAP	or	PAP or Training Race
	Monday		HIT	or	HIT
	Tuesday		rest	or	PAP
	Wednesday	REST			
	Thursday				
16–19	Friday		HIT	or	rest
	Saturday		PAP	or	HIT or Training Race
	Sunday		HIT	or	PAP or Training Race
	Monday		rest	or	HIT
	Tuesday		rest	or	PAP
	Wednesday		HIT	or	rest
	Thursday		PAP	or	rest
	Friday		HIT	or	rest
	Saturday		SPAM	or	Major Race
	Sunday		PAP	or	Race
	Monday		SPAM	or	PAP
	Tuesday		PAP	or	SPAM
20–26	Wednesday				
	Thursday				
	Friday	REST			
	Saturday				
	Sunday				

General training plan

The following training plan maps out a 23-week schedule. You will find the descriptions of the workouts specified in Chapter 9. On days without a specified resistance or bike workout, you should rest. Some of the rest periods are noted in the training plans below. In weeks 12-14, the Bike column follows a 3 days on/3 days off pattern, and the Alternate Bike column follows a 3 days on/4 days off pattern. Continue this pattern for the final 10 days of the training block.

WEEK	DAY	RESISTANCE	BIKE	ALTERNATE BIKE
1-3			LIP, MITO	
	Saturday	Hypert		
	Sunday		LIP, MITO	
	Monday	Hypert		
4-7	Tuesday		LIP, MITO	
	Wednesday	Hypert		
	Thursday	REST		
	Friday			
	Saturday	Strength		
	Sunday		MITO	
	Monday	Strength		
8-11	Tuesday		MITO	
	Wednesday	Strength		
	Thursday	REST		
	Friday			
	Saturday		HIT	HIT
	Sunday		HIT	HIT
	Monday		HIT	HIT
	Tuesday			HIT
	Wednesday			
12-14	Thursday			
	Friday		HIT	
	Saturday		HIT	HIT
	Sunday		HIT	HIT
	Monday			HIT
	Tuesday			HIT

WEEK	DAY	RESISTANCE	BIKE	ALTERNATE BIKE
	Saturday		HIT	
	Sunday		SPAM	
	Monday		HIT	
15-19	Tuesday		SPAM	
	Wednesday			
	Thursday	REST		
	Friday			
	Saturday		HIT	Race
	Sunday		PAP	Race
	Monday		SPAM	PAP or HIT
20-23	Tuesday		PAP	SPAM
	Wednesday			
	Thursday	REST		
	Friday			

TROUBLESHOOTING

When all is going well, training is easy. You feel good; you are recovering appropriately before your next workout; you easily are able to reach your target heart rate and power zones. After each workout, you are able to replenish your glycogen stores, and you are ready to tackle the events of the day.

Suddenly, you hit a bump in the road. You don't feel as though you have energy, and you are having trouble reaching the target training zones. Perhaps you are feeling the effects of an upper-respiratory infection (a cold) or are suffering from loss of sleep.

The different types of problems attributable to training are really different types of fatigue. Understanding the signs and symptoms of the effects of fatigue are important to ensure proper recovery.

PROBLEM SET #1: UNABLE TO REACH TARGET TRAINING ZONE...

...on the first attempt.
An initial failure to reach a target might occur during an interval session when you are not adequately warmed up. Often, a high-intensity warm-up is needed

for near-maximal effort.[1] If you try again and still cannot elevate your heart rate or power, there might be a more serious underlying problem. To evaluate how you are feeling, you must compare two performance values, such as heart rate and power or speed. If you cannot elevate your heart rate at all beyond zone 1, you are probably too tired to be training and should rest. If the fatigue persists, your physician should evaluate you.

If your heart rate goes to a certain level but not beyond—for instance, up to a heart rate training zone 3 but not to zone 4—evaluate the power you are producing. If the power is a normal level for the heart rate, diet is probably at fault. Be sure you are providing your body with the carbohydrate it needs to build glycogen stores. If the power is lower than normal, you could be flirting with overtraining and should rest for at least three days.

...on the second attempt.

If you have completed one or more intervals but are unable to do more, you have likely depleted your glycogen. You need to stop the workout and focus on glycogen stores by consuming 1 gram of carbohydrate and 0.3 grams of protein per kilogram of body weight. This should be consumed immediately after workouts and again at one hour afterward. I recommend carrying along an appropriate snack that you can eat as you start to cool down.

...on the third (or higher) attempt.

The rules for repeated failure to meet a target are the same as for the second attempt with one exception. If you are performing 8 reps of intervals on one day but can perform only 4 the next day, then glycogen might be the cause, or you might need more rest days. Different people need different amounts of time to adapt to training. If you are having trouble on day 3 of a training block, you can perform 2 days of exercise followed by 3 days off. This will help you adapt better to training and will make you stronger in the long run. To struggle through a set of intervals without reaching your target zones will only hurt your subsequent training. If you have exercised to the fatigue stage, it is time to focus on recovery so that you can come back stronger.

PROBLEM #2: YOU COMPLETE A WORKOUT BUT FEEL HORRIBLE FOR THE REST OF THE DAY.

Feeling terrible after a workout frequently happens to athletes who perform lipolysis or glycogen-depletion rides without replenishing their glycogen and protein afterward. Traveling with a blender to make smoothies isn't always feasible, so you need some other options. There are many commercially available soy- and milk-based shakes that have the correct ratio of carbohydrate to protein (3:1). Whether you store some at work or carry them while traveling, having recovery food with you will help you feel better after training.

PROBLEM #3: YOU ARE REACHING ALL OF YOUR TRAINING ZONES BUT ARE UNABLE TO PROGRESS OR INCREASE POWER.

When fatigue limits progression of training, you should consider overtraining as a diagnosis. Overtraining is a syndrome marked by staleness of training, depression, disrupted sleep, and frequent infections.

Symptoms of overtraining

- Earlier exhaustion during a constant velocity
- Decreased power during a maximal effort
- Increased time over a given distance at a constant heart rate
- Increased muscle fatigue
- Increased heart rate for a similar perception of exertion
- A variation in resting pulse
- Decrease in performance despite training
- Sleep disturbances
- Increased frequency of infection
- General feeling of staleness
- Irritability

The training methods in this book use the principle of overreaching as a way to push the limits of the body's capabilities. Without proper recovery, caused either by bad nutrition, poor sleep, or inadequate time off, overreaching can quickly become overtraining.

Some other symptoms and signs of overtraining include sore muscles, elevated resting heart rate, and decreased power at a given heart rate.

Once overtraining has set in, the treatment is rest. Adequate rest is important, and achieving it can take some time.

At this point, further training is out of the question, because even light exercise can make you feel tired and will not contribute to further fitness. Don't worry about losing any fitness that you have gained; the downtime should not result in significant decreases in training effect.

One way to ensure you are getting enough sleep is to assess how you feel when you wake up in the morning. If you awaken refreshed and feeling alert, you are well rested. If this is not the case, progressively accelerate your bedtime by 30 minutes a day until you awake feeling refreshed.

When you return to exercise, you should "start low and go slow." Try not to increase volume by more than 10% per week. Low-volume, high-intensity workouts are probably better because they can induce secretion of anabolic (muscle-building) hormones that will help your body repair itself.

An honest review of your training habits can alert you to the cause of the overtraining. Frequently, athletes skimp on adequate glycogen replacement because they are worried about staying lean. This strategy is faulty, however; the result will be muscle breakdown and weakening of the immune system.

PROBLEM #4: YOU ARE JUST FINISHING A REST BLOCK BUT STILL FEEL TIRED OR SORE.

Feeling tired or sore even after resting means you still need to rest. Cut the workout short and take another rest day. Try to resume the training plan the following day. If you are able to complete the workout, you should incorporate the extra rest day into your training. If you are unable to complete the workout because of fatigue, the overtraining syndrome might be the problem.

PROBLEM #5: YOUR POWER IS ADEQUATE, BUT YOUR ENDURANCE IS LACKING.

Low-intensity endurance is carried out primarily by the type I muscle fibers. These fibers are fueled by the circulating dietary glucose, stored glycogen, or fat. If you have been training the faster-twitch type II fibers, the type I fibers have been trained as well. The key to endurance exercise is fueling the type I fibers. This can be accomplished by increasing the use of fat as a fuel beyond the 12–20% that fat contributes to low-intensity endurance exercise.

One method of achieving this is to perform the lipolyis workout before doing other workouts. After you replenish glycogen, you can do the other workouts. The benefits of the lipolysis workout are increasing the enzymes needed to break down fat and getting the fat molecules into the mitochondria.

A high-fat, low-carbohydrate diet for five days will have a similar effect on the use of fat as an energy source for endurance exercise.

Performing glycogen-depleting workouts on the last day of a training block and following that with a low-carbohydrate diet for three days will also increase the body's ability to store glycogen.[2]

Maintaining adequate hydration with a dilute carbohydrate solution (5–8 grams of carbohydrate in 100ml of water) will also deliver enough fluid and fuel to the exercising muscle if taken at the rate of 500–1200ml per hour.

PROBLEM #6: YOUR LEGS FEEL TOO TIRED AND FATIGUED TO DO ANYTHING.

One way to lessen the effects of muscle soreness is to use postactivation potentiation (PAP). If you have sore muscles, perform 10 seconds of isometric leg extensions. The principle of isometric exercise is to apply force without moving your muscles. This can be done by trying to move a weight that you cannot lift. Several 10-second bouts of isometric exercise should help to decrease muscle soreness.

PROBLEM SET #7: YOU MISSED WORKOUTS.

Single missed workouts: Don't look back. Skip it and move on.

Multiple missed workouts

Less than 3 weeks: Because you have about 3 weeks of inactivity before detraining fully sets in, you should be able to pick up where you left off.

More than 3 weeks: After 3 weeks of inactivity, you will need to backtrack in your training plan. The last of the gains to leave will be strength and explosive power; the first gains lost will be the endurance benefits. Start with priming, mitochondrial, and lipolysis workouts before progressing to HIT intervals.

NOTES

1. A.M. Jones, D.P. Wilkerson, M. Burnley, and K. Koppo. 2003. Prior Heavy Exercise Enhances Performance during Subsequent Perimaximal Exercise. *Medicine and Science in Sports and Exercise* 35, 12 (December):2085–92.

2. P.M. Garcia-Roves, D.H. Han, Z. Song, T.E. Jones, K.A. Hucker, and J.O. Holloszy. 2003. Prevention of glycogen supercompensation prolongs the increase in muscle GLUT4 after exercise. *American Journal of Physiology, Endocrinology, and Metabolism* 85, 4 (October):E729–36.

INDEX